The Bethany We Know

Penny Roker is a Sister of Mercy of the Institute of Our Lady of Mercy Great Britain. She also is a member of the Institute's formation community in London. With experience both in teaching and prison chaplaincy, she now works as a counsellor and spiritual director. Previous publications include *Homely Love: Prayers and Reflections Using the Words of Julian of Norwich* (2006) and *At Home with God: How to Go on Retreat Without Going Away* (2009), published by Canterbury Press.

THE BETHANY We Know

Exploring Relationship in the Company of Jesus

PENNY ROKER RSM

VERITAS

Published 2016 by Veritas Publications
7–8 Lower Abbey Street
Dublin 1, Ireland
publications@veritas.ie
www.veritas.ie

ISBN 978 1 84730 684 5

10 9 8 7 6 5 4 3 2 1

All scripture quotations taken from the *New Revised Standard Version
Bible* Anglicised Edition copyright © 1989, 1995 Division of Christian
Education of the National Council of the Churches of Christ in the
United States of America.

A catalogue record for this book is available from the British Library.

Cover designed by Heather Costello, Veritas Publications
Printed in the Republic of Ireland by SPRINT-print Ltd, Dublin

*Veritas books are printed on paper made from the wood pulp of managed
forests. For every tree felled, at least one tree is planted, thereby renewing
natural resources.*

CONTENTS

Introduction

Some of the most touching episodes in Jesus' life took place in a hillside village just outside Jerusalem called Bethany. In some ways these were very ordinary encounters. The Gospel stories associated with this place tell of bickering sisters, weeping mourners and hungry travellers; of a donkey tied up to a street door and a fig tree with no figs; of disfiguring disease and arguments over money; of the joys of loving as well as the other emotions it can arouse. This Bethany is not a place that we will ever know, yet Bethany was and is like any other place in which we may find ourselves. It scarcely matters where it was or what it looked like: Bethany represents community in every place and age.

What made it special was that at one point in history Jesus spent periods of time there. Intriguingly, only St John's Gospel links Bethany with Mary and Martha. Saint Luke's vivid depiction of the two sisters places them vaguely in 'a certain village' (Lk 10:38). Perhaps he wanted to protect the villagers during what may have been a dangerous time for anyone associated with Jesus. Luke's evasiveness suggests that Bethany may have been a base for Jesus' ministry or even his home from home.

The precise location of the Bethany that Jesus knew is not conclusively established, although it is thought to have been in or close to what is now al-Eizariya on the south-eastern slope of the Mount of Olives, two miles from Jerusalem. Pilgrims still come here to see the tomb of Lazarus – it was the association with Lazarus that gives the place its name. Today al-Eizariya is an overcrowded Palestinian town, which has been occupied by Israel since the Six-Day War of 1967. The Israeli West Bank barrier has been built across its main road.

It would be satisfying to our human curiosity to be able to place Martha and Mary's Bethany more confidently. It would be more satisfying still to reconstruct it as it was when Jesus was there and to preserve it forever. But Jesus is not frozen in time. He is, depending on our beliefs, either long dead, executed by the Roman authorities two thousand years ago, or alive and risen, never again to be restricted to one time or place or circle or culture. In that sense, it should not matter all that much whether we can precisely locate Bethany on the map. Wherever we are, that is where he has promised to be.

This book does not say much about the original Bethany. How could it? Scripture references reveal tantalisingly little about life there at that time. The fragments we do have, however, are very precious for what they mirror back to us. What matters most is not piecing together the broken shards of the past, but allowing God to bring to our attention whatever gives meaning to our lives now. Like the feeding of the five thousand, it depends on what we do with how little we have. Approaching a few verses in the Gospels honestly and reflectively can go a very long way if we revere them and share them with others who hunger for insight. Our purpose is not to forget, to fossilise or to replicate the past, but to allow it to transfigure the present. Bethany need not be a memory for those of us who desire to meet Jesus in the ever-changing 'now'.

The location of Bethany is symbolic: it stood on the pilgrim route, yet slightly off the track; it was close to the busy city, yet out of view. A Bethany-kind-of-living must by definition be a liminal lifestyle, for Jesus continues to lead his disciples away from too close an identification with the 'world' in order that we might serve it better. This, to some extent, describes the life of a Sister of Mercy. Indeed, this book was originally inspired by a series of prayerful gatherings of Sisters of the Institute of Our Lady of Mercy Great Britain in preparation for their Seventh General Chapter in 2013.

What emerged from these meetings was the voicing of a desire for ongoing renewal of the community life that has always been at the heart of the Sisters' vowed life of poverty, celibacy, obedience and service of those in need. Christians living together as a joyful family are a sign and witness to the world of the love and mercy of Christ. It is an important aspect of the 'New Evangelisation'. Modelling healthy relationships is something of a mission in itself, reaching out to a world starved of security and love. The developed world seems to have forgotten who its 'neighbour' is. Children are hungry for attention; old people for community; partners for commitment. In the relentless pursuit of individualism, people experience the happiness of belonging and sharing less and less. Christians, by their love for one another, can be a beacon of hope to those for whom life has lost meaning. In both a material and spiritual way, Gospel communities provide shelter and nourishment, re-orientation and companionship to the needy, the wounded and the lost.

This, then, is essentially a book about relationship. Jesus' life in Bethany provides valuable insights for religious communities, church groups, work colleagues and ordinary families who want help with relational growth, conflict resolution or team building. The book may be used as a private reader for individuals who feel the need for some support and encouragement in their relationships; equally it can be used to facilitate the work of groups, whether they are newly formed and in the process of 'bonding' or well established but in need of renewal. Each chapter of the book provides suggestions for personal prayer as well as detailed guidelines for a group exercise, which may be attempted with or without the help of an outside facilitator.

Group dynamics can be complex. Until people come to forgive, to understand and to trust one another, no group can function effectively. Keeping channels of communication open and a willingness to engage are key to this. This book aims to make sharing as non-threatening a process as possible. It is recommended that those intending to use the book together as a group should commit to meeting regularly for an agreed number of sessions in order to tackle a chapter at a time. Each chapter stands alone so the group may decide to select a few topics appropriate to their own situation rather than to attempt to cover them all. It is recommended that each member takes time to read, absorb and reflect upon the chapter material beforehand.

Some balk at the investment of time and energy required in community building, others at the very real anxieties involved in personal sharing in a group setting. Any kind of change may seem daunting, especially when old ways of organising things or established areas of responsibility are called into question. Conflict is especially frightening, but for peacemaking to have any chance of success the voices of hurt must first be heard. People reluctant to meet because they already feel overstretched may be pleasantly surprised at how much new energy is released once old wounds begin to heal. It is important to gather together with an open mind, trusting in the whole group's wisdom rather than trying to steer people towards a preferred outcome, predetermined privately by a few. When those two or three gather instead in a spirit of unity, they will find the Christ in their midst to be as transforming a presence as the villagers of Bethany found him to be.

As God's chosen ones, holy and beloved, clothe yourselves with compassion, kindness, humility, meekness and patience. Bear with one another and, if anyone has a complaint against another, forgive each other; just as the Lord has forgiven you, so you also must forgive. Above all, clothe yourselves with love, which binds everything together in perfect harmony. And let the peace of Christ rule in your hearts, to which indeed you were called in the one body. And be thankful. (Col 3:12-15)

ONE

Friends Disguised as Enemies

*A man was going down from Jerusalem to Jericho, and fell into
the hands of robbers, who stripped him, beat him, and went
away, leaving him half dead. Now by chance a priest was going
down that road; and when he saw him, he passed by on the
other side. So likewise a Levite, when he came to the place and
saw him, passed by on the other side. But a Samaritan while
travelling came near him; and when he saw him, he was moved
with pity. He went to him and bandaged his wounds, having
poured oil and wine on them. Then he put him on his own
animal, brought him to an inn, and took care of him. The next
day he took out two denarii, gave them to the innkeeper, and
said, 'Take care of him; and when I come back, I will repay you
whatever more you spend'.* (Lk 10:30-35)

Bethany was at the end – or beginning – of one of the most
dangerous stretches of road in the Roman Empire. The road
dropped steeply as it wound its way down towards Jericho from
the temperate climate of the Mount of Olives. High rocks on
either side offered a perfect environment for bandits who might
appear from nowhere only to melt back into the cave-studded
terrain. With every step the journey grew hotter until the road
finally descended into the searing heat of the Jordan Valley.
Towards Jericho was a pass where travellers were particularly
vulnerable to attack. Here the rock was a natural blood-red
colour. It was an evocative landmark.

Jesus was familiar with this notorious road. In fact, one of
his parables described a journey along it. Since St Luke places

the parable of the Good Samaritan immediately before his story of the two sisters of Bethany, he might have assumed that Jesus was heading in that direction when he told the story. Jesus' imaginary scenario of a wounded traveller carried to an inn was by no means far-fetched. An old inn still stands along the way, designed in time-honoured fashion around a courtyard with a well in the middle. Though it was built by the Turks long after Jesus' day, it is almost certainly on the site of an earlier one. Any innkeeper along that road would have been known to Jesus and have chilling tales to tell.

Priests and Levites were also a common sight. Many priests lived in Jericho and travelled up to Jerusalem to offer the Temple sacrifices for a week at a time; Levites, too, went up and down to fulfil their traditional family roles as Temple officials. Travellers would group together for protection, and at festival time the road was thronged with pilgrims. Thus, Jesus found himself in company as he set off from Jericho, and one of his companions turned out to be a teacher of the Law. With the possibility of sudden death on many of their minds, the teacher, teasingly perhaps, asked of Jesus, 'what must I do to inherit eternal life?' (Lk 10:25)

Jesus turned the question around: 'What is written in the Law? What do you read there?' The teacher duly recited, 'You shall love the Lord your God with all your heart, and with all your soul, and with all your strength, and with all your mind; and your neighbour as yourself ...' but he was not so easily put off. 'And who is my neighbour?' he asked (Lk 10:27-29). This was more than the opening salvo of a philosophical debate. It was a legalistic question – one to which, if we are honest, we all hanker for a precise answer. To establish just how narrowly we are justified in defining our obligations to other people would enable us to pursue an essentially selfish course within the bounds of decency, untroubled by conscience and still in good standing with God.

Jesus' response rings through the ages, a precious legacy of that journey to Bethany for all who follow their own path towards right relationships. He told a story, possibly the most famous story in the world. Picture the side of this road, he seemed to be saying. Imagine over there a Jew left for dead after being attacked by bandits. A priest and a Levite pass him by but neither do anything to help him. Now, what if the only passer-by to offer him any assistance turns out to be a foreigner, an enemy ... someone from Samaria, perhaps? Which one then would be his neighbour?

The Jews knew all too well who their neighbours were, for Samaritans shared the same territory. Samaria was the area sandwiched between Judea and Galilee, though due to an ancient dispute the Jews felt nothing but loathing for its people. By choosing the hated Samaritan as a model of neighbourliness, Jesus challenged the kind of tribal outlook that limits our social responsibilities to those inside our social circle. He exposed the prejudices that lock us into negative assumptions about those we do not like, those notions and fantasies that justify our unwillingness to engage with them.

Like Jews and Samaritans of old, we too are prone to making enemies of our neighbours. Within our team, group or community there is likely to be someone who particularly irritates us, even someone we detest. They may even share with us a common territory, background or faith. Our instinct is to fight them or run from them. We may persuade ourselves that we owe them nothing, that they are not our problem, that it is safer to pass by on the other side. What we fail to appreciate is that they are very much our problem. They may even be the solution.

Love your enemies, Jesus urges us. They are a mirror to us. In them we may subconsciously recognise something of the most hated part of our selves. More than that, they will bring into the open the very best and worst of who we really are. It is easier to show love to those for whom we feel love, but to do good to someone we do not like requires an exercise of will. Loving one's enemy means transcending our natural inclinations. Jesus does not ask us to feel warmth towards our enemy, but to do the right thing by them and to accept that in some way he or she is a necessary part of the whole.

Often we will fail to obey Jesus' commandment to love; it is then that the pride, weakness or hard-heartedness within us is revealed. At last we glimpse beneath the exterior we present to the world to see ourselves as God sees us, stripped like the traveller in Jesus' parable. Robbed of anything to commend us, we can only abandon ourselves to God's unconditional mercy. For bringing us to this graced moment of self-honesty, we have every reason to bless our enemies.

Jesus strips everyone in this parable. At the beginning of his story we think we recognise the two 'sides' into which we habitually divide people: 'those like us' and 'those who are different' – 'the good' and 'the bad'. Jesus' companion on the road would no doubt confidently have placed the priest and Levite into the category of respectable people, and into the category of wicked people consigned all robbers, Samaritans and innkeepers.

Jesus, however, softens our perceptions. The characters begin to emerge from this parable as human beings really are – wanting to help but having responsibilities, resistances or livelihoods that can complicate the choices they make. We see the despised Samaritan administering first aid with great tenderness, but eventually having to entrust the wounded man into the care of another in order to get back on the road. We see the priest and Levite, not necessarily the heartless hypocrites we imagine, on their way to the Temple with sacred ministries to perform on behalf of the people – duties for which they must remain ritually 'clean' from any contact with the dead. As for the innkeeper, we see him treating injured wayfarers but making a good living out of it ... does that make him good, bad or somewhere in between? Jesus makes no judgement.

Gradually, our neat system of categorising people begins to break down. Certainties are dissolved until all we are left with is a sense that, though few are entirely selfless, all human beings have some goodness within them; that, despite first appearances, there is less to distinguish one from the other than we originally thought. We are all on a journey; everyone is wounded in some way, each needing the other if any of us are to make it to a refuge of safety, healing and recovery. Jesus seems to be encouraging us to swap the labels of 'good' and 'bad', even to remove them altogether. Do this with the characters in his parable and you are left with the kind of ordinary people you might expect to meet in any church group, team ministry or religious community.

Any group we have ever been a part of is likely to have the same kind of characters that we meet in the Parable of the Good Samaritan: Victims, Disrupters, Avoiders, Rescuers and Organisers. You may know someone who likes to play 'Victim'. He or she may not be as innocent as they appear; some people habitually blame others rather than take responsibility for their own choices. Helplessness and dependency bring their own rewards. Sympathy for a victim, however, can absorb the attention of a group and divert it from its real purpose.

We all know someone whose presence poses something of a threat. 'Disrupters' are to be found in every circle. They may not be bandits as such, but even respectable people can sometimes refuse to 'play by the rules'. Their intrusions and demands may threaten to rob the group of all it holds dear, yet their behaviour also allows members to feel a satisfying sense of self-righteousness, as well as giving them the opportunity to blame someone else for the group's lack of progress.

It is common for groups to have members who are reluctant to get too involved. 'Avoiders', like the priest and Levite, are afraid of making mistakes. Theirs may be a policy of 'no responsibility, no risk'. They flatter others into leadership instead, and the readiness with which others take the initiative at their prompting appears to justify their own inaction.

The 'Rescuer' or Good Samaritan will gain his or her reputation for virtue outside the group more than within it. Those closer to him or her may recognise in them a need to be needed, as they may unwittingly collude with the learned helplessness of others. By taking on more than they can cope with, they may leave other people with the real responsibility. They may also disempower those they are trying to support: compulsive helping can cushion people from much-needed challenge, or sabotage a natural process of relinquishing whatever hinders growth.

Every group needs an 'Organiser' like the Innkeeper. They may emerge as the group's natural leader due to their qualities of reliability and resourcefulness. Good at fixing things, however, they may leave other people feeling redundant, outshone or exploited; those they help may even be saddled with an uncomfortable sense of indebtedness. As a result, they may not always gain the approval they desire.

We have overlooked someone. Without a 'Mule' there would have been no rescue story at all. There is often a passive or silent member in any group. They may not be accustomed to decision-making nor even want any part in it, but he or she holds a great deal of power whenever they refuse to move forward.

There may be other roles that people play in your family or community. Most of us unconsciously learn or develop patterns of behaviour to get what we need. These continue throughout our lives, or until such time as they no longer serve us well. In a new relationship of more honest engagement they are no longer needed.

The tensions and dysfunctions of a group are far from being a disaster: within them lies an invitation. First, an unwritten rule must be broken, the one that says: 'You must become like us if you wish to belong.' It is in difference that any group's creative potential lies. If they sensed a greater belonging, for example, the 'Disrupters' might want to invest in the group instead of sabotaging it. Their unwelcome interventions might turn out to be much-needed challenges. What they threaten to rob from the group may eventually turn out to be a necessary 'letting go'. Likewise, if the contribution of the one who usually plays 'Victim' was sufficiently recognised, they might be less likely to resort to dependency and blaming.

'Avoiders' are afraid of being left alone with a responsibility they cannot handle, but if the group were less critical they would have less need to be cautious. The 'Organiser' would feel less put upon in a more fully participative group, offering their contributions less conditionally. The 'Rescuer' would have no need to court admiration or foster dependencies if they were to feel a sense of self-worth. Most crucially, where a collective vision begins to motivate people, silent obstructionism is no longer able to hold everyone to ransom; once they sense a shift in pace and purpose, the 'Mule' of the group will begin to move forward rather than risk being left behind.

It is not the group itself that creates the tensions – these are usually the result of old wounds. On the contrary, the group holds the key to growth and healing for each of its members and, more than that, a way of creating something greater than anything its individuals could possibly achieve on their own. In this sense, the Inn represents a transitional space where, in an environment of acceptance, people can begin their work of 'becoming'. Unless we receive from other group members the help we need to get there, we will, figuratively speaking, be left like the traveller in the parable: half-dead beside the road. Half-dead – half-alive – is how we may often feel in any group, but if Bethany represents healthier relating, then the Inn could be a significant stop along the way.

FOR PERSONAL REFLECTION

The 'Good Samaritan' Examen

-᛫- *During a short period of quiet reflection, think of someone in your life towards whom you feel anger or animosity. Thank God for him or her, especially for what God may be trying to teach you. Reflect, not just on how you feel at the moment, but upon what may lie beneath the feelings, such as past experiences or buried memories. Acknowledge whatever characteristics or behaviours the person brings out in you, both good and bad.*

-᛫- *Jesus said of the Samaritan that, when he saw the wounded man, 'he was moved with pity' (Lk 10:33). Be confident that Jesus' heart will be filled with compassion when he sees your vulnerability. Ask him to forgive you for any way in which you have failed to be a neighbour.*

-᛫- *Pray that tomorrow will bring the opportunity you need. How might you show that you are a neighbour after all?*

FOR A GROUP EXERCISE

⚜ *Allow an agreed period of quiet reflection for each person to consider how well you get on with the other members of the group:*

- *What does 'good neighbourliness' mean in practice as far as you are concerned?*
- *When have you experienced something less?*

⚜ *In a larger group you may wish to organise yourselves in pairs, changing partners after a few minutes until everyone has had a chance to share with everyone else. Resist the temptation to talk about anyone other than the person you are with. A smaller group may decide to stay together. It is important to be affirming as well as honest, but if you are comfortable enough to say if you have felt hurt, then say so.*

⚜ *When everyone has finished, rearrange yourselves in a circle and spend a moment in silence to honour and absorb all that has been offered in love.*

⚜ *We are told that the Good Samaritan bandaged the wounded man's wounds, ' ... having poured oil and wine on them' (Lk 10:34). Consider together: what is the 'oil and wine' this group needs to pour on its wounds?*

⚜ *Has any healing been experienced already?*

TWO

Free to Belong

Now as they went on their way, he entered a certain village, where a woman named Martha welcomed him into her home. She had a sister named Mary, who sat at the Lord's feet and listened to what he was saying. But Martha was distracted by her many tasks; so she came to him and asked, 'Lord, do you not care that my sister has left me to do all the work by myself? Tell her then to help me.' But the Lord answered her, 'Martha, Martha, you are worried and distracted by many things; there is need of only one thing. Mary has chosen the better part, which will not be taken away from her.' (Lk 10:38-42)

The Feast of Tabernacles, also known as the Festival of Booths or Shelters, took place at the time of year when the grape and olive harvest had been safely gathered in and the weather was still pleasant enough to camp out for the week-long festival. Constructing a temporary shelter out of branches and leaves was an important part of the festivities. It recalled the time when the Israelites were a homeless, wandering people. Escaping slavery in Egypt, they lived simply and trustingly from day to day, dependent on the unfailing provision of manna from God's hand.

It was during the so-called 'Exodus' trek from Egypt that the Jews had come to understand that God was inviting them to a special relationship with himself. Thus, the feast was foundational to their faith and often referred to as 'The Festival'. It was possibly the greatest of the three great feasts for which every Jewish male was required to journey to Jerusalem. Jesus would have been one of many pilgrims passing Bethany on the way.

It sounds as though the story of Martha and Mary recounted in Luke's Gospel might have taken place at this festival season. Here in Bethany, Jesus had found a place to stay just out of sight of the city, over the brow of the hill in Martha's house. Martha's family home no doubt regularly offered hospitality to pilgrims from the north. Since Martha later described her brother Lazarus as 'he whom you love' (Jn 11:3), Jesus had evidently become something of a family friend.

The Bethany story was set in the courtyard of Martha's house. It was here that the shelter of leafy boughs would have been erected. Given that Jesus was a welcome and familiar figure, it is poignant that St Luke recounts a sharp difference of opinion between Martha and her guest. Jesus was seated in the leafy shelter ready for the meal, with Martha's sister Mary at his feet, when suddenly the peace was shattered: 'Lord, do you not care that my sister has left me to do all the work by myself? Tell her then to help me' (Lk 10:40).

There is something heart-rending about Martha's protest, as though it were not the first or only time she felt left alone to do all the work. A lingering sense of injustice lies at the root of most relationship rifts. For many, the old wound may not be the way tasks are apportioned but simply a lack of appreciation. Unvalued and unrewarded, even the most generous-hearted can begin to feel like slaves.

Detecting the original cause of a sense of injustice may not be easy if the original grievance is disguised behind some other issue. Martha's outburst of irritation was triggered by embarrassment about the way her sister was behaving. The place of a woman according to the custom of the day was to wait on the men, not sit down with them to eat. Posing at a rabbi's feet like a rabbi-in-the-making was an exclusively male stance. Worse still, Jesus was encouraging her. He seemed to be saying that it was good for a woman to talk about spiritual matters, that it was only right for a woman to share fully in the feast. If St Luke or his sources fabricated the story of Mary and Martha, as some scholars believe, then it must have been characteristic of Jesus for the story to sound credible. This was certainly not the only occasion when Jesus challenged traditional ways of relating to women.

Martha would not have been alone in feeling uneasy about aspects of Jesus' teaching. He offered acceptance and belonging not just to people undeservedly marginalised, like lepers and Jewish women, but to 'wrong-doers' like robbers, prostitutes, tax-collectors and, in individual cases, even with the Roman oppressors. The concept of a Kingdom of God that afforded full membership to all comers scandalised as many people as it attracted. It overturned ideas about right and wrong that Martha had grown up to accept. The exchange of words between Martha and Jesus may even become a dialogue within our own heads, where the loftier idealism of Jesus tussles with a natural affinity for the harassed Martha. The law of love that welcomes the idle and the sinful into God's Kingdom meets with a very natural resistance at times, from all types of people. Jesus, however, expects us to transcend our deep-rooted instinct for justice with an all-embracing generosity characteristic of God himself.

Jesus' radicalism was not something new. The inclusive Kingdom he envisaged was rooted in ancient tradition. Zechariah had spoken of a time to come when the Jewish people and their enemies would sit down together at the Feast of Tabernacles:

Then all who survive of the nations that have come against Jerusalem shall go up year by year to worship the King, the LORD of hosts, and to keep the festival of booths ... On that day there shall be inscribed on the bells of the horses, 'Holy to the LORD' ... and every cooking-pot in Jerusalem and Judah shall be sacred to the LORD of hosts. (Zec 14:16, 20-21)

Thus, Tabernacles not only recalled the ancient past, it also heralded a glorious future where membership of God's family would be extended to all people. Then, even the humblest of daily objects would become holy vessels consecrated to the Lord. The feast was intended to be a joyous thanksgiving for deliverance, not, as it was in danger of becoming for Martha, a stressful cause of renewed captivity.

> *Rejoice during your festival, you and your sons and your daughters, your male and female slaves, as well as the Levites, the strangers, the orphans, and the widows resident in your towns. ... for the LORD your God will bless you in all your produce and in all your undertakings, and you shall surely celebrate.* (Deut 16:13-15)

There was a sense of immediacy in the way Jesus used ancient prophecy. Here, in Martha's kitchen, were those very cooking pots of Jerusalem. Martha, still locked in her own kind of slavery, appeared, perhaps, to exhibit the controlling, self-righteous and accusing attitude of the Israelites of old, whose crossing of the Red Sea was only the first stage of a much longer process of spiritual release. Jesus seemed saddened by Martha's refusal to enter into the spirit of the feast, and by her reluctance to sit at his feet with Mary to listen to his word. The command of Moses may have come to his mind:

> *... during the festival of booths, assemble the people – men, women, and children, as well as the aliens residing in your towns – so that they may hear and learn to fear the LORD your God and to observe diligently all the words of this law.* (Deut 31:10, 12)

Jesus was literally fulfilling this direction as he called Martha and Mary together to hear his teaching. In the calling of Martha's name we hear Jesus' deep desire for her to experience the new freedom and belonging that Mary was already discovering in his presence.

Not everyone is willing to become more fully a part of God's people or, indeed, of any group. There is comfort to be derived from licking the wounds of self-righteous indignation; it may feel better casting judgement from a safe distance. Staying where we are is a secure if unhappy option when the alternative is to lose face, risk disappointment or face challenge. One thing is for sure, no one ever becomes a new person by being censured or belittled for their failure to grow. People simply retreat behind protective walls. Disapproval makes us feel worse about ourselves, and attempts at self-reformation become short-lived. Love alone transforms. It is only when we feel accepted and valued that we dare to lower our defences and experiment with a different way of being. The key to our self-improvement is therefore held by those with whom we share our lives.

If we had been the one whom Martha publically scolded, who knows what sharp retort may have issued! Jesus did not react. There was no need to be defensive. 'Martha, Martha' (Lk 10:41) he said gently. He neither accused nor judged but simply observed that she seemed harassed, that she fretted about many things. The experience of being 'heard' can be very healing. Saint Luke does not tell us how Martha responded, but the gentle pleading of Jesus must surely have left her feeling not lectured so much as understood.

As for us, we too are invited, not just to listen more attentively to Jesus, but, metaphorically speaking, to sit at one another's feet as well. Now may be the time to stop accusing people and try hearing instead what they are saying or not saying. It may be time to engage directly with those who annoy us rather than grumbling about them to others. It may be time to emerge from the kitchen or office, or wherever tasks absorb our attention, in order to be fully present to those with whom we live, at least when it really matters. Like the Tabernacles or Shelters, the opportunity to enjoy one another's company may not last long.

It may even be time to consider whether we are in any kind of Egyptian exile of our own making, and whether the time has come to take up Jesus' offer of a more liberated quality of living. Perhaps by our efforts we are trying to convince ourselves of our own worth, but we might discover a less punishing way of working, less punishing for others and for ourselves. Then the horse's bridle, the cooking pots, the laptop, spanner or any other tools we use in our daily work can be offered up as part of the worship of our lives and, with us, take on a new sacredness.

Like the leafy shelters of the Feast of Tabernacles, it is possible to construct a way of life that reminds us of the way we used to be: closer to nature, dependent on God and journeying like pilgrims towards a better future. Our Promised Land, whatever that may mean for us in terms of relationships, may still seem a long way off, but we can still keep before us God's dream, a dream that is for all people and not just for the few. In our particular shelter – home, church or community – let no one feel that they belong any less than everyone else.

FOR PERSONAL REFLECTION

Martha's Prayer

- *Martha began her outburst with the words: 'Lord, do you not care that ...?' (Lk 10:40) When have you have felt like saying such angry words in prayer?*

- *Explain to Jesus how you feel. Hear him repeat your name as he repeated Martha's.*

FOR A GROUP EXERCISE

- *When Martha made her angry complaint, Jesus did not engage in counter-accusations or try problem-solving, nor did he submit to the pressure she was putting on him. Instead he calmly made an observation. Gather to consider how well the group functions. Agree beforehand how long you would like to spend on the exercise that follows.*

- *After a time of silence, invite each member in turn to make an observation about how your group is getting on. This should be done without naming or blaming any individual. You might find it helpful to begin with: 'I feel ...' or 'I notice ...' or 'I sense ...' Allow each person to speak without interruption. When everyone has had their turn, honour what has been said with a moment's silence.*

- *Jesus said to Martha: 'There is need of only one thing' (Lk 10:42). In light of what has been said, explore together: what one thing in particular does the group need at this time?*

- *Conclude with the following psalm. These verses are from the 'Songs of Steps', chanted by pilgrims as they made their way together up the winding road to Jerusalem:*

Unless the LORD *builds the house,*
those who build it labour in vain.

Unless the LORD *guards the city,*
the guard keeps watch in vain.

It is in vain that you rise up early
and go late to rest,
eating the bread of anxious toil;
for he gives sleep to his beloved.

Happy is everyone who fears the LORD,
who walks in his ways.

You shall eat the fruit of the labour of your hands;
you shall be happy, and it shall go well with you.

Glory be ... (Ps 127:1-2; 128:1-2)

THREE
The One Thing Needed

She had a sister named Mary, who sat at the Lord's feet and listened to what he was saying ... the Lord answered her, 'Martha, Martha, you are worried and distracted by many things; there is need of only one thing. Mary has chosen the better part, which will not be taken away from her.' (Lk 10:39-42)

There are precise expectations about the construction of a shelter for the Feast of Tabernacles. One is that the roof of leafy branches must only be very loosely woven. It is important to be able to see through it – to the stars.

I find this deeply moving. It is as though the weather-proofing of our dwellings has come to be symbolic of a growing impenetrability. We keep out not just the rain but everything in our lives that threatens to cause us discomfort or uncertainty. In the end we no longer know what it feels like to long for something or simply to wonder. The stars, mysterious and beyond our grasp, are obscured by the glare of cars and street lights. We forget what it is to stumble in the darkness: there is no need to reach out a hand.

For all our cleverness, we have allowed some of the most valuable things in life to be taken away from us, such as our faith life, meaningful conversation and closeness to nature. Trusting in providence seems laughable to a society saturated with excess. To a generation for whom communication has become both instant and constant, waiting upon God in contemplative prayer seems unendurable. People are both ever accessible and unavailable, for when it comes to the inner dialogue, to relationship and to prayer, many modern humans have simply 'lost the signal'. What is for us 'the better part'? A week in the shelter of leafy boughs under the stars might help us to answer that question. A break from the internet or from mobile phones might also help to remind us what is most important in our lives.

According to the sequence of events narrated by St Luke, Jesus' arrival at the house of Martha and Mary followed the sending out of seventy-two of his disciples to all the villages and towns with a message. They were told to say: 'The kingdom of God has come near to you' (Lk 10:9). When they first set out they may scarcely have understood the message they were proclaiming. On their return, however, they spoke in amazement of evil spirits banished by the power of Jesus' name. It was as if his disciples' eyes had been opened to a new reality, one that Jesus had always perceived, and their material world was suffused with a spiritual dimension beyond all imagining. Their more visionary Master, filled with the Holy Spirit, uttered in joyful ecstasy, 'I watched Satan fall from heaven like a flash of lightning' (Lk 10:18).

It becomes ever clearer that Jesus regarded his mission as something altogether more urgent than religious reform or the improvement of people's lives. He was intent on saving them from destruction. We sense his fierce impatience with people like the Pharisees who might have shared his zeal for righteousness had they not blindly obstructed him at every turn. It is unlikely that Jesus' dialogue with Mary in the leafy shelter in the courtyard of her Bethany house was either academic or superficial. The subject matter was – and still is – more important, more personal and more immediate.

We tend to be as naïve as the seventy-two disciples when it comes to all that invisibly surrounds us. Our attention may be taken up by inconsequential chatter, by the constant demands of other people, by the ephemera we consider so important.

It prevents us from fully appreciating everything that makes life meaningful. It also blunts our awareness of danger. Jesus knew God to be a loving presence; his Father's goodwill made everything else seem of little consequence. Satan seemed very real to him too – Jesus called him the Accuser. By setting himself up as the enemy of humankind, the Accuser was no longer at home in heaven, and every time we emulate his accusing work we are no longer companions of Jesus but instead are colluding with a hostile campaign to resist the coming of his Kingdom. Jesus must have felt frustrated and disappointed that good people like Martha could accuse her sister so vehemently when there was so much more at stake.

Martha was not necessarily any less spiritual than Mary. After all, she was the one who had 'welcomed him into her home' (Lk 10:38). However, welcoming Jesus is not enough – his presence demands our presence. Mary's lingering at the feet of Jesus was not a matter of presumption or indolence as Martha seemed to think, but one of listening obedience. It was not only the depth of Jesus' words that were so arresting, but also the earnestness of his message and the authority with which he spoke. While he was addressing her, nothing else mattered.

Some, reading the story of Martha and Mary, have conjectured that 'the better part' signified the superior calling of prayer over service, yet Jesus' own life was a balance of both. Jesus can only have meant that 'the better part' is to acknowledge the presence of God when he comes near; to put aside whatever else preoccupies us and to listen carefully to what he might be saying instead of venting our petty frustrations onto him. God does not demand our constant attention but he surely has prior claim to it.

The 'better part' is to bow to God's sovereignty rather than to assert our own. It was not that Martha's duties or her injured feelings were unimportant, but that stress had distorted her sense of what mattered most. Mary was drawn to a presence that put everything else in perspective. She spent time with Jesus, not only because she enjoyed his company – she seemed to relish every moment of it – but because it was as some translations have it, 'the right thing' (Lk 10:42). Mary listened to God because she was obedient – it was the right thing to do. She was not at the centre of her own universe but she sensed that Jesus was. She managed to see her own shaky construction of leafy branches against a glorious backdrop of stars.

Martha was not alone in failing to take Jesus seriously. Many of us, if we are honest, disregard the concept of spiritual warfare as if it were no more than the cultural expression of a bygone age. The dangerous influence of evil is not the only aspect of the spiritual dimension that we underestimate; we may scarcely be aware how near we are to the majesty of God. For the Israelites and their descendants, the presence of God in their midst during the desert trek was a powerful and abiding image. At the Feast of Tabernacles they remembered with joy how God had chosen to dwell amongst his people. The Book of Exodus recorded how God had instructed Moses to build him a dwelling place amongst humankind, which he called 'the tent of meeting':

I will meet the Israelites there, and it shall be sanctified by my glory; I will dwell among the Israelites, and I will be their God. (Ex 29:43-45)

We sense that Mary discovered that sheltering presence in the courtyard of her own home. There sat Jesus, God-with-us.

We too will meet God in a very personal way in our churches week by week; to receive Christ in Word and Sacrament is vital to our well-being. If we are to grow it is also important to spend regular time alone with God to read, to reflect and to pray by ourselves. Prayerful attentiveness and the ordinary activities of daily life are not meant to be in competition or in opposition to one another, though it can sometimes seem that way. Any reflective person can serve a meal and still notice the stars, but when he who made the stars wishes to address us directly, we do well to take off our apron and listen more intently.

Our capacity to listen is often impaired. So much distracts us from the sound of God's voice in our lives. Mary sat with rapt attention in the physical presence of Jesus. His words must have seemed compelling, his presence irresistible. For us, the daily time of quiet prayer may not always be an instantly gratifying experience. The 'better part' is not always the part we most desire. Mary, we are told, *chose* the better part, and for us it is even more an exercise of will. The reflective life requires us to cultivate receptivity within ourselves. Self-discipline is involved until habits of reflection are formed. The Kingdom of God is not likely to take any of us by storm; God will come close only when we open our hearts and minds to welcome him as Martha did 'into her home' (Lk 10:38).

It is easy to blame circumstances, but the biggest obstacle to a reflective life is usually our own disinclination. There is a Mary and a Martha within us all: a part that longs for the nearer presence of God, to sit wordlessly at his feet; and a part that always finds something else that requires our more urgent attention. Jesus' words to Martha must influence the choice we make each day; time with him is the 'one thing' needed and it must 'not be taken away' from us (Lk 10:42).

Daily time spent in solitude with God is one of the best ways to fit us for relationship. The success or failure of any kind of communal life hinges upon the spiritual maturity of its adult members, and upon their reflective capacity. Otherwise, we will weave the branches of our own little personal shelter too tightly, so to speak, for us to see beyond. To grow as a person by allowing the spirit of God to saturate our minds and hearts is to offer the group of people with whom we spend our time the precious gift of Jesus' own joyous, visionary presence. As we have already seen from St Luke's passage about Martha and Mary, it is a presence that engages with people, that empathises with their struggles, a presence that attracts, challenges and transforms. The daily practice of time alone with God starts to grow from a particular time in a particular place to become a whole new way of being in the world. It is not possible to experience sitting at the feet of Jesus each day and not be changed.

The shelter of leafy boughs, which Martha and Mary constructed in their Bethany courtyard, would have been taken down at the end of the seven-day Festival of Tabernacles, but my guess is that a different kind of tabernacle emerged for them instead, an invisible and interior one. Though Jesus took to the road again, leaving them to resume their ordinary lives, in a strange and wonderful way he remained right there with them. So it is for us.

There can be a tabernacle for Jesus at the very heart of each one of us, built like the leafy boughs of the Festival of Tabernacles out of whatever is to be found readily to hand. Jesus does not require us to buy or borrow from anyone else's spiritual store, but to make a home for him using what is already in us. What may appear a ramshackle dwelling will be the very place our Guest feels comfortable. Jesus' presence will make it holy.

FOR PERSONAL REFLECTION

The 'Tabernacles' Prayer

🔹 *The following psalm is traditionally recited at the Feast of Tabernacles. Still yourself before God and read the psalm slowly. Notice what arises or finds an echo in your own heart.*

One thing I asked of the LORD,
that will I seek after:
to live in the house of the LORD
all the days of my life,
to behold the beauty of the LORD,
and to inquire in his temple.
For he will hide me in his shelter

in the day of trouble;
he will conceal me under the cover of his tent;
he will set me high on a rock.
Now my head is lifted up
above my enemies all around me,
and I will offer in his tent
sacrifices with shouts of joy;
I will sing and make melody to the LORD. (Ps 27:4-6)

FOR A GROUP EXERCISE

🔹 *Meet to consider how well the group accommodates or nurtures the need of each individual to sit down 'at the Lord's feet' (Lk 10:39).*

🔹 *After a time of silence, invite each member to share how well the environment fosters their personal spiritual life. What do they need? What would they like to be different?*

🔹 *Allow each person to speak without interruption. When everyone has had their chance, honour what has been said with a moment's silence.*

- Then, remembering Jesus' clear directive that time with him 'will not be taken away' (Lk 10:42), explore together how the group may be able to support one another better.
- Conclude by saying the following psalm together:

O God, you are my God, I seek you,
my soul thirsts for you;
my flesh faints for you,
as in a dry and weary land where there is no water.

So I have looked upon you in the sanctuary,
beholding your power and glory.
Because your steadfast love is better than life,
my lips will praise you.
So I will bless you as long as I live;
I will lift up my hands and call on your name.

My soul is satisfied as with a rich feast,
and my mouth praises you with joyful lips
when I think of you on my bed,
and meditate on you in the watches of the night;

for you have been my help,
and in the shadow of your wings I sing for joy.
My soul clings to you;
your right hand upholds me.

Glory be to the Father and to the Son
and to the Holy Spirit,
As it was in the beginning, is now and ever shall be
world without end.
Amen. (Ps 63:1-8)

FOUR

The Prophet in Our Midst

*Then he entered Jerusalem and went into the temple; and when
he had looked around at everything, as it was already late, he
went out to Bethany with the twelve.*

*On the following day, when they came from Bethany, he was
hungry. Seeing in the distance a fig tree in leaf, he went to see
whether perhaps he would find anything on it. When he came
to it, he found nothing but leaves, for it was not the season for
figs. He said to it, 'May no one ever eat fruit from you again.'
And his disciples heard it.*

*Then they came to Jerusalem. And he entered the temple and
began to drive out those who were selling and those who were
buying in the temple, and he overturned the tables of the
money-changers and the seats of those who sold doves; and he
would not allow anyone to carry anything through the temple.
He was teaching and saying, 'Is it not written, "My house shall
be called a house of prayer for all the nations"? But you have
made it a den of robbers.'*

*In the morning as they passed by, they saw the fig tree withered
away to its roots. Then Peter remembered and said to him,
'Rabbi, look! The fig tree that you cursed has withered.'*
(Mk 11:11-17, 20-21)

If Jerusalem was the public forum in which Jesus faced the
hostility of religious leaders, Bethany offered a safe haven to
which he could withdraw when the day was done. To modern
eyes he appears to have been something of a commuter at festival
times. Down the stony track he went in the morning, and then

back up and over the ridge of the Mount of Olives at the setting of the sun. Anticipating another dose of taunts, testing, even ridicule, from men of influence as he taught in the Portico of Solomon day by day, perhaps the morning downhill trek felt equally 'uphill'. As every prophet has discovered to his or her personal cost, God's truth is not the kind of truth everyone wants to hear.

Jesus may have found a welcome amongst the villagers of Bethany, but it seems that he could not always count on being fed. The documented hunger of Jesus and his so-called cursing of the fig tree suggest that the Galilean wanderers generally lived a hand-to-mouth existence. Invitations to dinner, as well as food donations from well-wishers, appear to have been gratefully received, even the loaves and fishes of a child. Otherwise it seems to have been a case of scavenging from the roadside. The sight of a healthy-looking fig tree raised everyone's hopes as they left Bethany one morning for the city.

Bethany may have been renowned for its figs. Some have speculated that the place name derives from the Aramaic *bet hini*, meaning 'House of Figs'. That sweetest of fruits was one of the main fruit crops of Palestine, often dried and pressed into round 'cakes'. The first figs are a delicacy, appearing in March or April as little green knobs amongst the budding leaves. These tasty morsels were probably what Jesus was looking for. After growing to about the size of a nut they fall off to make way for the main crop. The proper figs or 'green' figs are harvested in August, though some do not ripen until after the leaves have fallen, so that even in the winter months the odd fruit is still to be found. Having lived much of his life in the countryside, Jesus knew what he was looking for. When he approached the fig tree it was in full leaf. He had every expectation of finding some tasty little buds unless, that is, someone else had got there first: 'there is no first-ripe fig for which I hunger ... there is no one left who is upright' (Mic 7:1-2).

It was a matter of concern if a fig tree should fail to live up to its promise. We learn from his parable of the fig tree (Lk 13:6-9) that farmers were reluctant to cut down a barren tree without first trying to stimulate it into production by digging in manure round its roots. The fig tree symbolised peace and prosperity. The disciple called Nathanael, whom Jesus first spotted in the shade of the fig tree, must have seemed the very picture of contentment. 'In days to come ...' said the prophet Micah, 'they shall all sit under their own vines and under their own fig trees, and no one shall make them afraid; for the mouth of the LORD of hosts has spoken' (Mic 4:1-4). This was how God intended it to be for all his children, a life of fulfilment, convivial and tranquil, secure in God's unfailing providence. For Jesus, steeped in the imagery of the scriptures, the budding fig could be closely associated with mankind's first innocence and bliss.

Food is for reflection as well as nourishment for the body, and we see Jesus using the fig tree in various parables and stories, just as other prophets had done before him. Prophecy is not necessarily about seeing into the future, it is more about being fully attuned to the here and now. The prophet experiences the same life events as everyone else but notices more: he or she is more aware of moral danger signs, more perceptive about people's true motives, more mindful of foundational values. As watchman for the community, the prophet does not speak on his own behalf, but proclaims what God reveals. That message is a call to change, whether a turning back or a moving forward. No wonder people both need their prophets and resent them: the prophet dares utter what all of us probably know in our heart of hearts but would much rather ignore.

Jesus experienced the same love–hate relationship that every generation has had with its prophets. He correctly predicted that rejection would be the ultimate outcome of his constancy to truth, yet he encouraged a prophetic stance in all his disciples, urging them to 'read' the signs of the times, to notice what may not be obvious to everyone, but what is nevertheless true and important for all to know. Before we rush to reject anyone in the group to which we belong, we should consider whether they might be a prophet in our midst. Could it be possible that unpalatable remarks, which we ascribed to their pettiness, may turn out to be a message of love from a very different source? So it was with Jesus. Religious leaders were outraged when he dared to claim that his words were given to him by his heavenly Father.

Like prophets of old, however, Jesus faithfully continued to deliver God's message by every means available, including the use of symbolic action. Saint Mark places the episode when Jesus overturned stalls in the Temple courts within the story of the shrivelling fig tree on the road from Bethany. Here we see dramatic gesture and imagery employed to drive home a point: the deceptive leafiness of a fig tree with no fruit was a vivid picture of the nation's religious life. He was not the first to use a barren fig tree to voice God's passionate regret at the nation's sterility. As Jeremiah had cried: 'When I wanted to gather them, says the LORD, there are no … figs on the fig tree' (Jer 8:13). Jesus pressed the analogy further: he cursed the fig tree. In doing so, he was not losing patience with a tree but desperately trying to warn an unrepentant people.

Jesus had not always despaired of Israel's religious leaders. As a boy he could hardly bear to tear himself away from his dialogue with teachers of the Law. The Temple was his Father's house, and he revered it, as did every Jew, as the most sacred place on earth. He identified with it in referring to his own death: 'Destroy this temple, and in three days I will raise it up' (Jn 2:19). One can only imagine how deeply scandalised this devout Jew must have been to see Temple worship through adult eyes. The profitable sale of sacrificial animals in the court of Gentiles lined the pockets of some at the expense of poorer people. With moneylenders luring people into debt and traders filling the porticos, the Jewish Temple was far from being 'a house of prayer for all the nations' (Mk 11:17). The offering of the widow's mite had touched Jesus deeply. It was probably not the presence of moneychangers or traders that disturbed him so much as the hypocrisy of ritual punctiliousness when blatant social injustices went unchallenged.

That morning, as Jesus anticipated his return to Jerusalem, the fruitlessness of the fig tree must have stood as a powerful symbol. Like the tree's deceptive leafiness, the piety of Jewish leaders and the Temple ceremonial grandeur seemed little more than outward show. Generations of prophets had failed to reform Temple life and now the zeal of God's own Son was meeting with fierce resistance. When Jesus said, 'May no one ever eat fruit from you again' (Mk 11:14), he was expressing heartache more than hunger. He was not out to destroy anything, neither Temple nor fig tree. On the contrary, he had pleaded with Jerusalem to avert the destruction it was bringing upon itself:

> Jerusalem, Jerusalem, the city that kills the prophets and stones those who are sent to it! How often have I desired to gather your children together as a hen gathers her brood under her wings, and you were not willing! See, your house is left to you desolate ... When he was sitting on the Mount of Olives, the disciples came to him privately, saying, 'Tell us, when will this be ...? (Mt 23:37-38; 24:3)

The disciples, it seems, were no more alert to the barrenness of their nation's faith life than the religious leaders themselves.

Mesmerised by its magnificence, they were perhaps too naïve to see that Temple life was already dying.

For those of us trying to cultivate life together in a church, marriage, community or group, it may be just as hard to see what is really going on under the surface. Sometimes we are simply too closely involved with day-to-day routines to notice signs either of growth or of decay. Just as the Temple in Jerusalem was a wonder of the world, we may be blinded to reality by the continuing admiration of onlookers. Jesus' fig tree was full of leaf, after all, when he predicted its demise. The crucial determinant, of course, was its fruitfulness or lack of it, and this is no different for us. Jesus said:

> *Beware of false prophets ... You will know them by their fruits. Are grapes gathered from thorns, or figs from thistles? In the same way, every good tree bears good fruit, but the bad tree bears bad fruit. A good tree cannot bear bad fruit, nor can a bad tree bear good fruit. Every tree that does not bear good fruit is cut down and thrown into the fire.* (Mt 7:15-19)

A leafless fig tree in winter might still bear a ripe fig or two to sustain a hungry traveller, so we need not look too critically at appearances. It is not the smartness of our buildings or the size or age profile of our membership that determine the health of a group. It is the fruit that counts.

It sometimes happens that, by imperceptible degrees, a group formed for mission may simply have become an end in itself. This may be due to its lack of new members. The pressing needs of an aging membership can make self-maintenance a higher priority. Older members may feel a painful sense of redundancy, whilst younger members struggle to manage. Sometimes the mission is handicapped by the very success it once enjoyed; complacency or nostalgia for some illusory golden age make people backward, if not inward-looking. Mutual recrimination, tiredness and a feeling of futility can gradually sap our energy and sense of purpose. Outward appearance begins to take on greater importance.

Thus, Jesus brings the fig tree to the attention of us all. He encourages us to notice what is really going on, not just around us but within us too, to be both honest and brave in engaging with truth. Jesus often referred to the 'looking but not seeing' attitude that cushions people from uncomfortable realities. Instead of rehearsing a wishlist that confirms us in a fantasy world of our own making, prayer life requires a listening stance so that we may be gently awakened to whatever inner resistances we may have. A daily personal conversion of our own must precede any of the changes we desire in other people. Openness – hollowness, even – is the necessary condition of one who receives and communicates God's words.

The prophetic voice, however, will be silenced within those for whom the approval of others is more important. Truth, as we may perceive it, is not always what others want to hear; people stoned the prophets of old. It was Peter who remarked, as the disciples walked back down into Jerusalem with Jesus, that the fig tree they had examined the day before in Bethany was not healthy after all, it was actually shrivelling up: 'they saw the fig tree withered away to its roots' (Mk 11:20). Peter was learning to see beyond outward appearances.

He had still, perhaps, to understand that the vitality Jesus was more concerned about was theirs – and ours – not that of the tree. It is a mistake to assume that prophets are all, by definition, prophets of doom. Through them God is calling us to life, to a quality of living that is within our grasp. 'From the fig tree learn its lesson,' Jesus urged his disciples, 'as soon as its branch becomes tender and puts forth its leaves, you know that summer is near' (Mt 24:32).

FOR PERSONAL REFLECTION

The Fig Tree Prayer

*'... he was hungry. Seeing in the distance a fig tree in leaf, he went to
see whether perhaps he would find anything on it ...'* (Mk 11:12)

⚜ *Where is there a hunger in you?*

⚜ *In what places have you been looking for something to nourish
yourself? Have you been successful?*

⚜ *Ask Jesus to help you find the 'sweetness' you need to sustain
your spiritual life at a hard time, or some 'out-of-season
delicacy' for the next stage of your journey.*

FOR A GROUP EXERCISE

*'Then he entered Jerusalem and went into the temple; and when he
had looked around at everything ... he went out to Bethany with
the twelve.'* (Mk 11:11)

⚜ *Bethany was very close to Jerusalem, but it was outside the city.
There, Jesus could rest in the company of his friends and co-
workers. A little distance enables us to see things in perspective.
Plan a retreat day with your group away from your home or
place of work, somewhere you can reflect on your situation in a
safe and relaxed setting. Begin and end it with a time of prayer
together. Build in opportunities for time alone, as well as time
to talk.*

⚜ *Do not try to force any outcome from this day – just be grateful
if something does emerge. Perhaps things will begin to look
different or a little clearer. Perhaps the pause will enable you
to see what you need to do. At the very least, the break from
your usual routine and the opportunity for companionship may
nourish you.*

FIVE

Discernment: A Way of Being

Then they tried to arrest him again, but he escaped from their hands. He went away again across the Jordan to the place where John had been baptising earlier, and he remained there. Many came to him, and they were saying, 'John performed no sign, but everything that John said about this man was true.' And many believed in him there.

Now a certain man was ill, Lazarus of Bethany, the village of Mary and her sister Martha. Mary was the one who anointed the Lord with perfume and wiped his feet with her hair; her brother Lazarus was ill. So the sisters sent a message to Jesus, 'Lord, he whom you love is ill.' But when Jesus heard it, he said, 'This illness does not lead to death; rather it is for God's glory, so that the Son of God may be glorified through it.' Accordingly, though Jesus loved Martha and her sister and Lazarus, after having heard that Lazarus was ill, he stayed two days longer in the place where he was. (Jn 10:39–11:6)

Earlier in his Gospel, St John tells us that this place across the Jordan was called Bethany (Jn 1:28). It suggests that there were two villages called Bethany. One we have already encountered on the Mount of Olives close to Jerusalem where St John says that Martha, Mary and Lazarus had their home. The 'other' Bethany was more than a day's journey away: it was here that Jesus went to seek refuge after things became too dangerous for him in Jerusalem. Martha's message came *from* Bethany *to* Bethany.

That 'other' Bethany on the far side of the Jordan, to which St John's Gospel alludes (Jn 1:28), was well known to Jesus because his cousin John had baptised there. It may have been where Jesus himself had come to receive Baptism at the start of his own public ministry:

> *And just as he was coming up out of the water, he saw the heavens torn apart and the Spirit descending like a dove on him. And a voice came from heaven, 'You are my Son, the Beloved; with you I am well pleased.'* (Mk 1:10-11)

The Gospels relate that the Baptism of Jesus was a transformative moment, awakening him to a sense of his true identity and life's purpose. It was something he was to experience again at the Transfiguration and Peter, who witnessed it, understood the importance of rekindling the memory of such moments: 'I think it right, as long as I am in this body, to refresh your memory ... we had been eyewitnesses of his majesty ... We ourselves heard this voice come from heaven' (2 Pt 1:12-18).

To know that he was unconditionally loved seems to have given Jesus the affirmation all human beings need and never tire of hearing. It is all too easy to allow circumstances to smother the sense of who we are and to dim the vision; the message of God's love for us is a 'holy memory' that illumines such moments of self-doubt or confusion. At difficult times we would do well to recall how, in some interior way, we too once 'heard' the assurance of God's abiding favour.

Three years had perhaps passed since Jesus was baptised by his cousin John. John was now dead, beheaded by Herod, and Jesus himself was now in acute personal danger. He had only narrowly escaped being stoned to death in Jerusalem by an outraged crowd who took exception to his claim to be God's Son. Having eluded the angry crowds in the Temple, he left Jerusalem, crossed the Kidron Gorge and climbed the track up and over the Mount of Olives. Swiftly descending the road towards Jericho, he crossed to that other Bethany on the far side of the Jordan. After a sweltering and dusty trek, he would eventually have reached the place where John had so recently been preaching and baptising.

The precise location of that 'other' Bethany is difficult to determine because the river has changed course over the centuries. Jordanian archaeological discoveries suggest that John may have been baptising not in the Jordan itself but in the plentiful pools of the Wadi Al-Kharrar on the other side of the river across from Jericho. The fresh water pools were close to the river crossing. They were fed from mountain springs that flowed into the River Jordan. It was an oasis of palm trees, tamarisk, reeds, grasses and shrubs beneath the very mountain where Elijah was said to have ascended to heaven in his fiery chariot.

This was an evocative place. John the Baptist, with his wild appearance and his cave at the foot of Elijah's mount, had seemed to be the prophet Elijah come back to life. Now that Jesus was performing miracles, surpassing anything that John had done, it was as if he were a second Elisha inheriting a double share of Elijah's spirit. After painful recent experiences in Jerusalem, the people's limitless belief in Jesus in this place may have provided the reaffirmation he needed.

It was while Jesus was seeking refuge in this welcoming and safe oasis that the news of Lazarus' illness arrived. Martha and Mary's message introduces an almost unbearable tension into the narrative, yet Jesus' response to it, 'This illness does not lead to death; rather it is for God's glory' (Jn 11:4), no doubt prompted the messenger to return with false hopes of Lazarus' recovery. We can almost hear the relief of the disciples too at Jesus' decision to remain where he was. Have we not all at some time chosen to understand the words of Jesus in ways that suit us? Lazarus' sisters trusted that Jesus would make their brother better; the disciples trusted that Jesus would keep them safe. The burden of other people's often conflicting and unrealistic expectations is one with which some of us may be familiar.

The sisters had not demanded that Jesus should return with the messenger; their message merely stated that Lazarus was sick, yet there was an implied sense of obligation. It reminds us that the greater pressure in such situations often comes from within: we are the ones to impose the highest demands upon ourselves; our choices may reflect an anxiety about retaining people's approval. When one person's need competes with another's – as Martha's 'Come!' and the disciples' 'Stay!' seem to do – then it is common to feel pulled in different directions.

Mostly we comply with the most demanding voice. In that sense we do not make choices at all, but simply jump through whatever hoops are placed before us. What we see in Jesus, however, is a glorious freedom from any urge to comply with people's expectations. He did not allow himself to become agitated by their disappointment. Though he was neither unmindful nor contemptuous of their feelings, he remained unswervingly obedient to the will of his Father.

To know what the Father is asking of us requires sensitivity to the movement of the Spirit. It is a mistake to think that discernment is the same thing as decision-making. Decision-making may be little more than weighing up pros and cons; discernment is a response to life. God's will is not so different from our own deepest desire, it just takes a while to become attuned to the heart's echo. We must also become attentive to the sources of wisdom around us, especially to scripture and to the lessons of our own experience. We have to quieten our busy minds if we are to catch what the prophet Elijah described as the 'still small voice' (1 Kgs 19:11-13). In that sense, discernment cannot be understood as a time of reflection or even as an extended period of preparation before an important decision. Discernment is a listening way of life.

It therefore comes as less of a surprise that, on receiving Martha and Mary's message, Jesus should stay where he was for a further two days. We detect no impulsivity in Jesus, nor any compulsiveness in yielding to pressure. His calm detachment dismays those of us with little trust in the benignity of a future in God's hands, and who require immediate answers to urgent needs. Jesus enjoyed the inner peace of one beloved of his Father. He trustingly surrendered all into God's hand, including those he loved.

Jesus' perspective can restore our own appreciation of life when we trust that God loves us. To allow God sovereignty in our lives is give up the need to try to impose our own control over people and events. We need no longer interpret every trying circumstance as disastrous. We can take time to reflect, to dialogue and to pray rather than panic, worry and rush. What we do, we will do better. What we have, we will enjoy more. Few situations require an immediate response or a knee-jerk reaction.

To borrow from the analogy of the 'other' Bethany, whenever our privacy and need for solitude are becoming eroded, Jesus invites us to a place on the far side of familiar territory. There we can make ourselves unavailable for a while and dare to be unresponsive to urgent calls upon our attention. When we do return to face the stresses of life – as Jesus also had to do – we may find that serenity is not just a place to retreat to, but a way to be. The protective haven, refreshing pools and ancient wisdom of that 'other' Bethany can be located within us all.

Jesus did eventually resolve to cross the river and go back to that other more dangerous Bethany on the outskirts of Jerusalem.

It seems that the two-day delay was significant to the Gospel narrative, and not just to make the raising of Lazarus appear all the more miraculous. Jesus may have been characteristically unhurried. Perhaps he needed a day or two longer to immerse himself in that evocative landscape and soak in the prophetic message of Elijah and John. Perhaps he was hearing God's call through the voices of more ordinary people who came to him there, those who were saying with amazement that, 'everything that John said about this man was true' (Jn 10:41). Perhaps Jesus simply needed time to relive the moving experience of his own Baptism, when God claimed him as his only beloved Son. The decision to go to Lazarus was not the reflex action of a compulsive helper. Jesus made a choice; it came from an inner freedom.

We too need time to remember and reclaim the original vision of own particular group or way of life when the pressures of life threaten to swamp it. Our sense of identity may have been shaped by the inspirational example of individuals of whom we are the spiritual successors. Of equal importance are those touchstone experiences of our personal faith journey. As Jesus discovered in that 'other' Bethany, the memory of who we are and what we are missioned to do must be rekindled from time to time if the addiction to pleasing people and habits of automatic responding are not to rob us of any will of our own. Ultimately we will fail to satisfy the urgent, multiple and often conflicting voices of insistence. However legitimate the need, we can only serve others by obeying God first; we can only ultimately fulfil what others want of us by remaining authentically who we are.

Jesus asked of his closest companions, 'But who do you say that I am?' (Mt 16:15). It suggests that the intimate group in which we find ourselves plays a crucial role in helping each of us in our personal work of becoming. Revisioning is important and it may require us from time to time to retreat to some place 'on the far side' of our present circumstances. If so, it may not be to seek fresh spiritual experiences so much as to remind ourselves what we already know to be true.

FOR PERSONAL REFLECTION

The Oasis: A Guided Meditation

Imagine yourself in a bustling ancient city. You are preparing for a journey in great haste.

- *What is forcing you to leave? (pause)*

- *Shouldering your bag and with a staff in your hand, you struggle against the flow of people and mules through the narrow streets. Eventually you come to a gate in the city walls. You leave through the gate, cross a bridge and, with the sun in your eyes, scramble up the slope of a hill. Breathless, you reach the top and pause to take a look at the city behind you before setting off along a twisting dusty road that steeply descends on the other side.*

- *As the road drops down, you notice how fiercely the heat intensifies. On each side you are dwarfed by high rocks. It feels as though there are hostile eyes watching you as you go through narrow passing places. You call out to them ... what is it that you want to say? (pause) The voice echoes round and round.*

- *Gradually, as you journey downhill, the weight of your luggage begins to feels lighter and lighter until you find yourself walking with greater freedom and less fear. The steepness of the descent lessens. The staff no longer seems necessary and you let it drop from your hand. The road has begun to widen out and reveal vistas to delight the eye – the glint of light on water far beneath you, hazy purple mountains on the horizon beyond, a distant citadel on a rock, a city laid out far below.*

- *After some time you approach a river. You know that it is important to cross this river because on the other side you will find the rest and safety that you long for, but something within you makes you hesitate to cross. What is it? (pause) You scramble down to the stream of dark water and find that it is shallow enough to wade across.*

- *As you emerge on the other side you see can see green vegetation ahead. There at last is the place you have been longing to find: pools of water shaded by palm trees; the scent of tamarisk in the breeze. You lie down to rest and cup the cool spring water in your hand to drink. (pause) This oasis is a place deep within you. 'Rest' in it. (pause) Whenever bad news comes or disputes arise, this is a place you can return to whenever you wish.*

Repeat slowly:

> *God is a safe place within me. There no one can do me harm.*
>
> *God is a green place within me. There I can revive.*
>
> *God is a known place within me. There I can remember who I truly am.*
>
> *God is a warm place within me. There I know with certainty that I am loved.*
>
> *God is a beautiful place within me. It draws to me those who value what I do and say.*
>
> *God is a timeless place within me. There departed ones live on to affirm and inspire me.*

FOR A GROUP EXERCISE

*'He went away again across the Jordan to the place where
John had been baptising earlier'* (Jn 10:40)

- *Agree together how long you would like to spend on this exercise.*
- *Take some personal time for reflection. Go back in your minds
to the time when you first became a part of this group, or when
it first formed. What was the original vision? Who or what
inspired you? What experiences shaped you?*

  *Return to the group and allow each person a few minutes to
share their memories with the others.*

' ... the sisters sent a message to Jesus' (Jn 11:3)

- *What 'message' or news or development may be prompting
this group to re-examine who you are and where you should be
going?*

' ... it is for God's glory' (Jn 11:4)

- *Jesus welcomed challenge and adversity as an opportunity to
glorify his Father. What possibilities for good can you envisage
in your own situation?*

SIX

Life-Giving Opportunities

Then after this he said to the disciples, 'Let us go to Judea again.' The disciples said to him, 'Rabbi, the Jews were just now trying to stone you, and are you going there again?' Jesus answered, 'Are there not twelve hours of daylight? Those who walk during the day do not stumble, because they see the light of this world. But those who walk at night stumble, because the light is not in them.' After saying this, he told them, 'Our friend Lazarus has fallen asleep, but I am going there to awaken him.' The disciples said to him, 'Lord, if he has fallen asleep, he will be all right.' Jesus, however, had been speaking about his death, but they thought that he was referring merely to sleep. Then Jesus told them plainly, 'Lazarus is dead. For your sake I am glad I was not there, so that you may believe. But let us go to him.' Thomas, who was called the Twin, said to his fellow-disciples, 'Let us also go, that we may die with him.' (Jn 11:7-16)

It had been two days since Jesus received an urgent message to tell him that Lazarus was ill, but St John tells us that Jesus stayed where he was at this oasis in the desert on the far side of the Jordan. His disciples seem to have been relieved to remain in a place of relative safety. Jesus' sudden resolve to return to Judea made them understandably agitated. There was little to fear amongst the villagers where his dear friend Lazarus lived, but if Jesus reappeared anywhere in the Jerusalem area it would soon come to the attention of the same angry Jews who, only a short while ago, had been trying to stone him to death. The disciples expressed their consternation in no uncertain terms.

I like to imagine that it was late afternoon when their discussion took place. Perhaps it was as the sun was sinking in the sky, casting long shadows, that Jesus made his enigmatic comment about the twelve hours of daylight. Every little stone and indentation along the path would be thrown into sharp definition as the sun dropped lower in the sky. A traveller in those days would cherish every bit of daylight left to him before darkness made it impossible to journey any further. In ancient times, in the absence of street lights, you could not attempt much in the way of walking or working at night time.

This image of the fading light was a graphic way of describing the creative potential within the final phase of Jesus' mission, and the importance of making best use of what time remained. Even in its last rays – *especially* in its last rays – the setting sun had the power to light up the traveller's way, but once the sun had sunk below the horizon it very quickly became too dark to do anything. It was a powerful metaphor for what were likely to be the last months of Jesus' ministry.

Saint John seemed to be saying that once our lifespan, which is allotted by God, has run out, nothing can extend it. However, so long as God has gifted us with life it should not be wasted in fear or given up on prematurely. Jesus continued to work right up until he fell into the hands of his enemies; he used what little time he had to the fullest extent. While the light of Jesus was still illuminating their understanding of God's world, the disciples needed to learn and grow. Confident of God's love for him, and in an attitude of abandonment to the will of his heavenly Father, Jesus did not see himself as courting danger; on the contrary, it seemed unnecessary for him to foreclose prematurely on his public ministry while there was even one hour of 'daylight' remaining.

His response to the precarious situation in which he found himself, and to the sad news of Lazarus' illness, offers us a glimpse of Jesus' unique and prophetic perspective. Whilst warning of impending doom, as the prophets before him had done, Jesus could also see the glorious possibility of God's coming Kingdom in the events unfolding around him. Like John the Baptist, Jesus expected some kind of disaster to befall the nation, yet he saw everything through the lens of hope. Even his stark pronouncement of the death of his dear friend, which had such a gloomy finality about it, offered an opportunity not to be wasted. He wanted to open the disciples' eyes to see God's unfailing goodwill towards humankind, especially towards those whom poverty, death and disease seemed to have marked out as sinners. He must have believed that God intended to transform the tragedy of Lazarus into something life-giving. Unconcerned about his own future, one which he knew was safe in God's hands, Jesus rejoiced: 'For your sake I am glad I was not there, so that you may believe' (Jn 11:15).

Gladness and confident hope are not emotions that usually accompany human struggles; in fact it may seem as though Jesus is very often 'not there'. Our own group, team or community may have experienced illness, death or opposition as the disciples did. We may share Jesus' sense that time is running out. Far from being glad, we may feel miserable and hopeless, anxious or afraid. We may agree with the disciples that it is best to stay safe. A sense of defeat can make us disinclined to try anything new; we may even want to give up altogether. Many groups become paralysed by the apathy of those members who prefer to grumble about problems than use that energy to initiate change. Like all charity, 'raising the dead' begins at home; we may need to start by recognising what is dead within ourselves.

It is difficult for any of us to acknowledge with complete honesty our resistance to other people's suggestions and ideas. We prefer to rationalise inaction with arguments such as: 'It's too risky'; 'We've tried that before and it didn't work'; 'It's too late'; or 'We shouldn't meddle with nature'. Some people may even derive a perverse kind of gratification from failure if it assigns them the role of tragic hero.

We can detect these same positions in the Gospel passage. Some disciples argued against going to see Lazarus because of the risk: 'Rabbi, the Jews were just now trying to stone you, and are you going there again?' (Jn 11:8) Assuming that Lazarus had dropped into a deep sleep, others were in favour of letting nature take its course: 'Lord, if he has fallen asleep, he will be all right' (Jn 11:12). Thomas – loyal, long-suffering and pessimistic – said with a melodramatic flourish, 'Let us also go, that we may die with him' (Jn 11:16).

Jesus neither indulged in heroics nor drew back in cowardice. He simply said, 'Our friend Lazarus has fallen asleep, but I am going there to awaken him' (Jn 11:11). Challenging death in this way must have appeared delusional. We have all met those who, by talking assertively, try to convince themselves of a control over events that they do not have, but this was neither bluster nor grandiosity on Jesus' part. He was not seduced by the sensation-seeking crowd. What we are hearing is the voice of a man with a uniquely transparent faith in God.

It is difficult for us to conceive how completely Jesus surrendered his mind and will to his Father. Faith for him was more than self-confidence, much more than a trusting nature; his degree of courage and conviction could only have come from an utterly transformative personal experience of God that dispelled fear. Whether God willed that Lazarus should die or recover did not disquiet him; the identification of his own will with that of his heavenly Father relieved him of all anxiety and of any need to try to control events or manipulate people. Thus, Jesus enjoyed an inner calm, his outlook framed by the expectation that God would be faithful to his promises. He could rest in that. Empty of self-interest, devoid of subterfuge, he was exactly as the Gospel writer described him: 'full of grace and truth' (Jn 1:14). Grace and truth shone out of him.

This statement about the twelve hours of daylight was not the first time Jesus had used the imagery of light. Saint John's Gospel tells us that he used it quite unselfconsciously to describe himself. At the Festival of Tabernacles, four enormously tall candelabra were raised in the Temple Court of Women, blazing with such light that every courtyard in the city was illuminated. It was perhaps while this was happening that Jesus made his ecstatic utterance above the crowd: 'I am the light of the world. Whoever follows me will never walk in darkness but will have the light of life' (Jn 8:12). It was a ceremony that recalled the Exodus from Egypt, when the escaping Israelites were led out of captivity by the pillar of fire. Jesus was claiming to be no less than that same divine presence, guiding and saving not just the Jewish nation but every human being who ever lived.

Our own glow may, by contrast, seem dim, even partially extinguished. We may recognise in ourselves a cynical hopelessness that characterises the 'darkness' of this world. We do not want to try again because the risk seems too great and our inertia too stultifying, but by our stubbornness we are resisting the movement of God's spirit, which prompts us to return to relationships that need healing. Jesus' description of a bright world of creativity and journeying being overtaken by the night is especially disturbing if we feel that we ourselves are contributing to the gloom. The cycle of twelve hours of daylight and twelve hours of darkness may describe how it is for many of us: spiritually speaking, we were once wide awake but have since fallen to dozing.

The metaphor of light and dark can also be applied to the way we perceive one another. Anyone who has searched for candles during a power cut will know how objects are drained of colour in the dark; shapes seem grotesque and frightening. We bump into things. The morning light transforms the scene: what once was a painful obstacle turns into something familiar and valued. So it is with one another. 'I can see people,' said the blind man to Jesus, 'but they look like trees, walking' (Mk 8:24). We are all half blind when it comes to the other people in our lives. The negativity we perceive in them is often no more than a projection of our own self-loathing. We judge by appearance and cling to initial impressions. We may experience new people as universally threatening because of our own insecurities. As a result, our view of the other can be distorted and unreal.

Community holds the potential to shine a light on the way we act as individuals in relationship. It challenges and exposes the prejudices, fears and competitiveness we hide even from ourselves. It enables us to appreciate how much more there is to know about a person and to begin to love what previously we could not see at all. Just as two eyes are needed to see three-dimensionally, so our appreciation of the whole person can be enhanced by more viewpoints than ours alone.

With the metaphor of the twelve hours of daylight, however, Jesus seems to be using the image of light in a specific sense to mean life-giving opportunity. The opportunity for forgiveness and healing may not last indefinitely. Shrinking from people we fear, avoiding people we dislike, putting off reconciliation with those whom we have argued with, is to stay on the far side of the Jordan in a safe oasis where everyone is warmly disposed towards us and where we do not have to make much effort with relationships. It is tempting to stay there indefinitely rather than cross into hostile territory. We do not relish the uphill struggle to re-engage with people who do not like us or whom we detest: people who question or intimidate us; people who see us as a threat and refuse to hear what we are trying to say. It does not seem worth the risk or effort. We may even regard a certain relationship to be as dead as Lazarus and take the view that nothing more can be done to save it. Jesus, however, persists in the hope that the relationship is dormant and that it may yet be 'awakened'.

Notice that Jesus did not order his disciples to go back with him to Judea. There were evidently some disciples who were not keen to follow him back into hostile territory. We may know people who are equally reluctant to leave their 'comfort zone' in favour of a more challenging form of relating. Encouragement of the more hesitant disciples came from an unexpected source. It was 'doubting' Thomas who rallied them: 'Let us also go' (Jn 11:16), he said. Thomas took the pessimistic view that Jesus' ideas were doomed to failure, but he was loyal enough to go along with him anyway. I wonder whether we too, acknowledging our reluctance to try something new, might dare to leave our safe 'oases' and re-engage with those whom we have given up for dead?

FOR PERSONAL REFLECTION

The 'Twelve Hours' Examen

'Are there not twelve hours of daylight?' (Jn 11:9)

⚜ *This is a bedtime prayer that looks back over the previous daylight hours. Where has there been 'light' in this day – things that have warmed you, enlightened you, sparkled for you, brightened your mood? Thank God for each moment. Where did you 'stumble'? How did that feel? Refrain from persecuting yourself. Instead, ask Jesus to shine a gentle light so that you can understand what went wrong.*

⚜ *Jesus said in response to Lazarus' death, '... for your sake I am glad ... so that you will believe ...' (Jn 11:15). Pray that whatever* has gone wrong today might be used by God for some good purpose.

✢ In order for this day to draw to a close in peace, what is it that you need to believe? What is it that you need to ask?

✢ Pray for the gift of healing sleep.

FOR A GROUP EXERCISE

✢ Read aloud the Gospel passage given at the beginning of this chapter. Which of the following images from the passage best describes your group at the moment?

a. In a healing sleep

b. Needing to be woken up

c. Walking in broad daylight

d. Stumbling in darkness

e. Dead

- The five choices should be written up on a flip chart or board, and each member of the group allowed an agreed time for personal reflection before writing A, B, C, D or E anonymously on a blank piece of paper (given out at the beginning).

- Draw the chairs into a circle and gather the folded pieces of paper. One member should examine them and reveal the results. Pause in silence to honour what has been expressed.

✢ Decide how long you would like to spend on the next part of this exercise.

- How do members of the group feel having heard these answers?

- If the answers seem unsatisfactory, how does the group desire to be?

- What do you need to believe in order for that to happen?

- What prayer seems to be emerging?

SEVEN

Engaging with Anger

When Jesus arrived, he found that Lazarus had already been in the tomb for four days. Now Bethany was near Jerusalem, some two miles away, and many of the Jews had come to Martha and Mary to console them about their brother. When Martha heard that Jesus was coming, she went and met him, while Mary stayed at home. Martha said to Jesus, 'Lord, if you had been here, my brother would not have died. But even now I know that God will give you whatever you ask of him.' Jesus said to her, 'Your brother will rise again.' Martha said to him, 'I know that he will rise again in the resurrection on the last day.' Jesus said to her, 'I am the resurrection and the life. Those who believe in me, even though they die, will live, and everyone who lives and believes in me will never die. Do you believe this?' She said to him, 'Yes, Lord, I believe that you are the Messiah, the Son of God, the one coming into the world.'

When she had said this, she went back and called her sister Mary, and told her privately, 'The Teacher is here and is calling for you.' And when she heard it, she got up quickly and went to him. Now Jesus had not yet come to the village, but was still at the place where Martha had met him. The Jews who were with her in the house, consoling her, saw Mary get up quickly and go out. They followed her because they thought that she was going to the tomb to weep there. When Mary came where Jesus was and saw him, she knelt at his feet and said to him, 'Lord, if you had been here, my brother would not have died.' When Jesus saw her weeping, and the Jews who came with her also weeping,

*he was greatly disturbed in spirit and deeply moved. He said,
'Where have you laid him?' They said to him, 'Lord, come and
see.' Jesus began to weep. So the Jews said, 'See how he loved
him!' But some of them said, 'Could not he who opened the eyes
of the blind man have kept this man from dying?'* (Jn 11:17-37)

It must have been with heavy hearts that Jesus and his disciples
struggled up the steep road to Bethany. Perhaps there were
lingering hopes among them that Lazarus might still be alive or
that the hue and cry for Jesus had died down. As they approached
Bethany, however, they must have heard the wailing of grief and
noticed a suspiciously large number of mourners had gathered
for the funeral.

In those days it was regarded as a religious duty to attend a
burial or at least follow the bier for part of its way to the tomb.
The more respected the deceased, the more mourners were
likely to join the procession. Burial took place within hours of
a death, but it was followed by a formal period of mourning
lasting seven days. During that time the family did not wash
or wear shoes and loud expressions of grief were orchestrated
by professional mourners. Friends and neighbours provided
food and accompanied them, wailing, in frequent visits to the
tomb. Community can be a supportive presence at such a time.
The numbers of mourners in Bethany who had come up from
the city, however, suggested that the real attraction was the
unfolding drama surrounding Jesus. People evidently expected
him to reappear at such an emotional time.

Public intrusion into private sorrow is, as we all know,
unhelpful if insincere, especially when the sorrow stems from
some friction between individuals. When an argument takes
place in public it may not always be easy to manage the outcome.
At worst it will become a dangerously exposing arena where the

taking of sides and whispering behind backs may push already distressed people into entrenched or isolated positions. At best, however, a group or community can provide a safe, non-judgemental and accepting space in which individuals can express uncomfortable feelings and reach a greater understanding of one another than they had before.

Despite the crowd of inquisitive outsiders looking on, the family setting in Bethany provided such an environment. When Martha and Mary took issue with Jesus over his late arrival, neither their sense of betrayal nor the unwanted publicity that surrounded them managed to drive any kind of wedge between Jesus and his friends. On the contrary, relationships were deepened. This Gospel narrative, as well as offering deep spiritual insights, models how to relate in an honest, open way so that conflict need not prove destructive.

It is sad that someone's death should lead to any kind of conflict between people; a funeral, however, can often become the setting for a family dispute. The issue for Martha and Mary was that Jesus, despite being a close family friend, had not been there when they most needed him. The sense of betrayal was all too evident. Each sister vented the same feelings, 'Lord, if you had been here my brother would not have died' (Jn 11:32). People around them voiced it more forcefully, 'Could not he who opened the eyes of the blind man have kept this man from dying?' (Jn 11:37)

It must have been very painful for Jesus to meet with such universal condemnation. Most of us behave defensively when criticised. Whether or not we are at fault, we may deny, excuse or apologise for our behaviour in order to placate the aggrieved party. Others, when criticised, take the offensive by making counter-accusations or feigning outrage; they may even refuse to accept that the other has any right to complain at all. Jesus was unusual in the way he received criticism. He used no armoury to dodge or deflect attack, neither did he retreat nor retaliate. We see in him only patience and self-restraint. He seemed prepared to feel the full sting of opposition. Uniquely, he placed the survival of his relationships above the inviolability of his own reputation. Rather than run, hide or disengage he stayed with the distress – his own and others'.

It is interesting to see how Jesus bore Martha and Mary's anger. It seems important to say 'bore' rather than 'dealt with', 'handled', 'coped with' or 'managed', for anger is not necessarily something to be contained or made safe. It is not in itself antisocial. Jesus had no need to be afraid of Martha's disappointment any more than he was by the tempest on the Sea of Galilee. Anger is within the range of normal emotions; it always has a cause and it may be justified. Expressing it in appropriate ways is better than nursing it.

It is only when someone feels that an issue has been 'heard' and understood that their anger subsides. Disputes are fuelled and prolonged by the other's refusal to accept or take seriously what they are saying. Jesus listened to Martha and Mary's complaint without countering or denying anything. That requires real humility and inner freedom. It is not the same as giving in or admitting fault, for the sense of being wronged may only be a perception. Empathy, which demonstrates that a person appreciates how it feels for another person, is almost always healing.

If Jesus was humble by listening without any counter-argument, he was also honest. He showed his feelings. The Gospel writer relates how upset Jesus was at his loss of Lazarus and, possibly, by the accusations that were being levelled at him. He was unable to see Mary cry without breaking down himself. Notice how strongly it is stated: 'When Jesus saw her weeping, and the Jews who came with her also weeping, he was greatly disturbed in spirit and deeply moved' (Jn 11:33). Then, 'Jesus began to weep' (Jn 11:35), openly enough for the crowd to make comments. To a generation brought up to interpret incarnate divinity as superhuman strength, the emotional vulnerability of Jesus comes as something of a shock. We expect God to be aloof and dispassionate rather than affected by what we feel. We may even prefer a God who rushes to take away someone's pain, as we might do, rather than one who shows solidarity with us in our sadness by feeling it himself. The 'fix-it' god is no more than an idol of our own making, modelled on our own inability to bear one another's distress.

Group tensions, however, will not be solved by practical and instant solutions unless there has first been some genuine acknowledgement of how people may be feeling. Anyone who has experienced communal sharing at a meaningful level will know how difficult it is to be self-revealing or face criticism from those whose good opinion matters. The easier option is to avoid honest encounters and keep one's feelings to oneself. In the long run, however, truth is more liberating.

Martha is an inspiration to all of us who desire to be real. Just as Jesus was open about his feelings, she was straightforward in confronting him with hers. There was no game playing in this exchange, no 'acting out'. We see no turning of backs, coldness or avoidance of eye contact – no pretence or disguises. 'When Martha heard that Jesus was coming, she went and met him' (Jn 11:20) and made an immediate statement of dissatisfaction. Mary, on the other hand, 'stayed at home' (Jn 11:20). Jesus had to take the initiative by asking for her before she too was able to express how she felt.

It is important to notice that however wounded they were by Jesus' apparent neglect, Martha and Mary observed a level of respect that might astonish a modern reader. In our own days of social informality, it takes less time to slip from easy familiarity into verbal abuse. A group may need to establish boundaries that can be 'policed' when the expression of differences of opinion goes beyond what is acceptable. It is nevertheless important not to stifle dissent nor push it into whispering corners; someone feeling hurt needs to be heard. Martha and Mary stated plainly what they felt without diminishing the other person: 'Martha said to Jesus, "Lord, if you had been here, my brother would not have died. But even now I know that God will give you whatever you ask of him"' (Jn 11:21-22). Mary repeated the same words: 'Lord, if you had been here, my brother would not have died' (Jn 11:32) and, as she said so, knelt at his feet in reverence.

Aggrieved parties should feel able to express their feelings directly, but without insult. Martha, at least, did not avoid, punish or reject Jesus, but kept the lines of communication open and allowed him to offer his own perspective. The relationship was by no means jeopardised by the honest exchange that followed; on the contrary, it deepened what Martha knew and valued in Jesus:

> Jesus said to her, 'Your brother will rise again.' Martha said to him, 'I know that he will rise again in the resurrection on the last day.' Jesus said to her, 'I am the resurrection and the life. Those who believe in me, even though they die, will live, and everyone who lives and believes in me will never die. Do you believe this?' She said to him, 'Yes, Lord, I believe that you are the Messiah, the Son of God, the one coming into the world.' (Jn 11:23-27)

If only our own deepest disappointments in life might give rise to such new hope; if only the times when our own friends let us down could become occasions of fresh affirmation and valuing.

The exchange deepened Martha's understanding of Jesus; it may even have deepened Jesus' understanding of himself. 'I am the resurrection and the life' (Jn 11:25), was a moment of self-revelation that arose not from a cosy relationship but out of the tension of loving challenge. Its implications for the good of humankind were limitless.

Where there is an audience, however, we are more likely to avoid the honest encounter, to pretend nothing is wrong, to feel pressurised by other people's expectations into being unduly aggressive or submissive. As in Bethany it is not always easy to find the necessary privacy. With so many people in the house, every word, action and gesture of Mary and Martha was likely to be overheard and commented upon. Jesus therefore remained on the outskirts of the village: 'When she had said this, she went back and called her sister Mary, and told her privately, "The Teacher is here and is calling for you." And when she heard it, she got up quickly and went to him. Now Jesus had not yet come to the village, but was still at the place where Martha had met him' (Jn 11:28-30).

Our own group may need to question how intrusive it can sometimes be, for example, to use other people's dramas for salacious gossip. The appropriate place for the group as a whole to talk through difficulties between individuals that affect everyone is not clandestinely in corners. Groups need a protected space where they can regularly 'check in' with one another, a time and place for honest encounters, where tensions and feelings can be explored and safely expressed within confidential boundaries, where loving challenges can be offered and misunderstandings cleared up. Such sharing is often known as 'group process'. Where unprocessed tensions have deadened relationships, group work of this kind has the potential to reconcile, restore and re-energise. It can bring a group back to life. The Lazarus story in St John's Gospel provides a good example of a source of tension successfully processed in the context of a trusting relationship. A non-threatening name for 'group process' might be 'Lazarus time'.

As Jesus and Martha discovered in each other's company, moving from the 'I' to the 'We' is a process, an ongoing work in which the experience of being together can facilitate not only mutual esteem but greater self-awareness and self-valuing for its individual members. It would be a shame if a community's tensions were seen as no more than differences to be 'buried'. A group merely 'kept ... from dying' (Jn 11:37) by avoiding conflict may find, by actively engaging with it, something infinitely more life-giving than that.

FOR PERSONAL REFLECTION

The 'Angry with God' Prayer
'Jesus saw her weeping' (Jn 11:33)

✦ *Mary, we are told, was slow to respond to Jesus' arrival. Eventually she hurried to him on the outskirts of the village, fell to her knees at his feet, poured out her complaint and wept freely. She then took Jesus to see where her brother had been buried, and it was seeing Mary's distress that made Jesus also begin to weep.*

  - *Find a place where no one else can see or hear you. Imagine Jesus waiting for you. In your heart at least, kneel at the feet of Jesus. Take a few moments to do this.*
  - *Tell him what you think has come between you. Share with him how you feel.*
  - *Escort him in your mind's eye to the place of your loss, anxiety or trouble.*

Imagine Jesus, seeing your distress, break down in tears. Allow him to weep for you. See how he loves you.

FOR A GROUP EXERCISE

'Lazarus Time'

✦ *Pull the chairs into a circle for a time of sharing together in the group. Decide how much time you would like to spend and appoint a timekeeper. First of all, discuss what is needed for this to be a 'safe' space where people can freely express what they need to say. You might like to agree on a few ground rules. After someone in the group has read aloud the Gospel passage from the beginning of the chapter take a few minutes of quiet time to consider how well each of you deals with conflict. Do you:*

a. *'Go to meet it' straightaway, like Martha.*

b. *Shrink from it, as Mary seemed to do, and have to be coaxed into saying what's wrong.*

c. *Talk about the issue behind the scenes, as the mourners did.*

d. *Find an appropriate time and place to talk directly to the person concerned, as Jesus did.*

e. *Other.*

- *Let each member of the group consider which of the above best describes their own pattern and how well this works for them.*

- *When everyone is ready, some members may feel able to share with the rest of the group. Other members of the group may wish to respond. It is important, however, that you leave sufficient time for the following final part of the exercise.*

Martha said: 'I know that God will give you whatever you ask of him.' (Jn 11:22)

- *Discuss together: what is it that your group is asking of God?*
  - *Finish with a time of prayer to offer requests to God, either aloud or in silence.*

EIGHT

The Power of Love

Then Jesus, again greatly disturbed, came to the tomb. It was a cave, and a stone was lying against it. Jesus said, 'Take away the stone.' Martha, the sister of the dead man, said to him, 'Lord, already there is a stench because he has been dead for four days.' Jesus said to her, 'Did I not tell you that if you believed, you would see the glory of God?' So they took away the stone. And Jesus looked upwards and said, 'Father, I thank you for having heard me. I knew that you always hear me, but I have said this for the sake of the crowd standing here, so that they may believe that you sent me.' When he had said this, he cried with a loud voice, 'Lazarus, come out!' The dead man came out, his hands and feet bound with strips of cloth, and his face wrapped in a cloth. Jesus said to them, 'Unbind him, and let him go.' Many of the Jews therefore, who had come with Mary and had seen what Jesus did, believed in him. (Jn 11:38-45)

Those who have come to think of Jesus as a composed and slightly aloof figure will not recognise him in this passage. The phrase 'greatly disturbed' (Jn 11:38) is a mild way of translating a Greek word that conveys a sense of snorting or shuddering vexation. The word has a sense of fierceness about it. His desperation, exasperation – whatever he was so intensely feeling at that moment – eventually found voice in a prayer of thanksgiving and faith, which culminated in the shout of 'Come out!' to Lazarus as its triumphant 'Amen'. How, after that, could we ever doubt that God cares? The raw material of miracle and of prayer, it seems, is none other than the agony of loving.

How different from the apparently calm detachment Jesus showed when he first received the news of Lazarus' illness! There he seemed indifferent and slow to act as we sometimes imagine God to be; here we see Jesus groan in the depths of his being. Amidst the desolate sense of loss and the turmoil of Jesus' feelings, a dead man staggers out of the dark void into daylight. It is as though the very moment of Creation is being replayed before our eyes.

Saint John understood that in Jesus we see God. This was not God as ancient people imagined him to be, his power demonstrated angrily in acts of destruction, but God as Jesus knew him and showed him to be, one who loved with intensity and recreated untiringly. The raising of Lazarus was one of seven 'signs' and in this last and greatest of the signs St John portrays Jesus as a deeply caring human being capable of doing what only God can do: bringing forth life.

> *He was in the beginning with God. All things came into being through him, and without him not one thing came into being. What has come into being in him was life ...* (Jn 1:2-4)

Jesus' indescribable disturbance in the depths of his being seems to be more than grief for the loss of Lazarus, and more than a reaction to the reproaches of those around him. It was, perhaps, anguish at their reluctance to accept that he was sent by God, and at their incomprehension of God's ways and rejection of God's love. Their unbelief agonised him. We do well to consider the extent to which we too have cooperated with or frustrated God's purpose, which is not to deprive us of joy but to offer each of us a spring of life bubbling up within. It may be that we have played some part in blocking the life-giving potential brought to us by those with whom we share our lives. If we are followers of Jesus, however, then we willingly accompany him back to the tomb scenes of our failures in the sure belief that nothing is so damaged as to be abandoned, no relationship so dead that it is unsalvageable.

Four days dead to an ancient Jew meant that the man's spirit had departed, for his face was now too far gone to be recognised. No wonder the place where Lazarus was raised to life became an early place of pilgrimage. You can still visit the site which ancient tradition identifies as Lazarus' tomb. It is on the slope of the Mount of Olives in the village of al-Eizariya, which takes its name from him. The settlement presumably grew around the tomb and so must have been close to, if not in the very place, where Bethany once stood.

There is nothing out of the ordinary about the sunlit modern street in which Lazarus' tomb is situated until, that is, the pilgrim steps through a door and down a twisting flight of worn stone steps to an ancient subterranean chamber in the rock. This is not the tomb itself – the burial chamber lies below. You enter it through a narrow aperture in the floor once covered by a stone. The aperture is just big enough to admit one person at a time. Squeezing through you enter the burial chamber itself. There the corpses were laid to rest in niches to await nature's depredations. After a year or so, what remained would be collected into small bone boxes and re-buried. Damp, and still with a pervading stench of death, the chamber is not a place to linger. It was from this very tomb, or one like it, that Lazarus was said to have struggled into the light, his hands and feet still separately bandaged, and his face tied in its own cloth. Unable to see, we imagine him blindly fumbling in response to the familiar voice of his friend crying: 'Lazarus, come out!' (Jn 11:43)

Most of us who read this story do so with a mixture of horror and disbelief. If our first thought is, 'Did this actually happen?'

then incredulity and suspicion shroud our view like the linen that bound Lazarus' face. There are more urgent truths than whether or not the raising of Lazarus was a historical event. Indeed, the story St John was writing was not Lazarus' so much as my story and yours. He hoped, perhaps, that our immediate response might be a fresh vision of God's purpose for those he loves, and a joyous desire to seize hold of life.

For all the medical advances that prolong our days, the fundamental question, 'What *is* life?' remains only partly answered, yet we do feel more 'alive' at certain times than at others. We sense that life must be more than the sum of our present troubles, and imagine a dimension beyond this biological framework in which we breathe and move. Some of us may already enjoy a spiritual life, which makes heaven feel close and incarnates the Spirit of Jesus right here where we are. Lazarus occupies that place of transition between death and life, between this world and another. To respond as he did to the voice of Jesus is not just to cross over into 'the life to come' but to embrace life more fully in the here and now. Knowing that Jesus offers a transfigured quality of living, what holds us back from accepting it? It is probably the same thing that held back the generation of Martha and Mary: unbelief.

The unbelief of others made Jesus something of a lonely figure. Even his nearest and dearest lacked any comparable experience of God. This passage in St John's Gospel is all about belief. It was a belief that had nothing to do with naïve credulity, and was far more than a mental 'check list' of dearly held values. It was even more than making religious observance a way of life. Faith is to discover what God is really like and to let that truth radically affect everything we do or think. Jesus believed in a God who does not show his greatness by smiting people down; instead, 'the LORD has redeemed Jacob, and will be glorified in Israel' (Is 44:23).

It was in God's saving power that he believed; saving was what he unhesitatingly expected God to do.

Verses 39 and 40 in St John's account of the raising of Lazarus stand as a pair of opposing perspectives. When Jesus ordered them to remove the stone, Martha objected: 'Lord, already there is a stench' (Jn 11:39). To this Jesus replied, 'Did I not tell you that if you believed, you would see the glory of God?' (Jn 11:40). These encapsulate two very different outlooks on life. Martha's statement represents the common belief that what has happened before is how it will always be; it assumes the prevalent hostility of everything around us, including nature and even, at times, God. Jesus' belief was not in the predictability of events but in God's compassion. Believe the truth that I am telling you, says Jesus, and you will discover for yourself what kind of Father he is!

The source of his faith was God himself and not his own reasoning. Jesus' knowledge of God was through personal experience. His trust in the indissolubility of his relationship with God left him unfettered by social anxiety and feeling rich in his poverty. He was desirous only of what was important to his Father, and of his Father's reputation. Nothing else was of such consequence. The continuous experience of the divine presence infused everything. For Jesus, it was the impossibility of living after dying that was the fiction, a time-locked way of thinking that wrests sovereignty from God and denies that his love for us is too strong to let us go.

As for Martha, the only things possible were the things she had already experienced. She was a prophet like ourselves, recalling the worst in order to set limits on what we dare hope for, a prophet whose vision was clogged with destruction. Jesus, the true prophet, may or may not have seen any further into the future but he clear-sightedly perceived God to be our Father. Though he saw the same signs of doom in the world about him as we do, it turned him not to despair but again and again to the source of unfailing mercy. Filled with the very nature of God, Jesus could do 'far more than all we can ask or imagine' (Eph 3:20). That seemed to include holding onto a sense of glorious possibility in the midst of death.

How closely faith is allied to hope and love! Faith is to encounter the same world as everyone else but to experience it differently: every bush burning, every flower arrayed as Solomon, every sinner a saint in the making. Faith transforms our perception not only of what is but makes us more trusting of what is to come; faith is not a closing off to otherness so much as an opening out to embrace 'beyond'. If we could believe that God is stronger than all we fear, and really take in the Good News of God's favour towards humankind, then we might delight in life as though it were the first day in Eden.

Life to the full is not a life that we may enjoy in isolation. Where broken relationships are concerned, however, many people prefer to remain outside the 'tomb' with the weeping Martha than to reclaim their 'dead'. 'Take away the stone,' Jesus cries! But we recoil from too close an inspection of whatever may cause unbearable feelings of shame or regret, guilt or fear. Jesus wept and still weeps because we cannot believe. Groaning with our pain he prompts us to re-engage with relationships that seem hopelessly beyond resurrection. Lazarus was not shocked back to life by a bolt of lightning from heaven, but awakened by someone whose voice he knew, a friend who loved him enough to enter with him into the most dreaded place. Jesus leads us back into the vault of painful memories and old prejudices. He stays close as we face the revulsion, fear and sometimes unwelcome publicity that accompany any first step towards reconciliation.

This resurrection story of Lazarus speaks of the transformative potential of relationship. It reminds us of the importance of beginning again – and again – when things go wrong. Where else but in an environment of complete acceptance, such as a family, a religious community or some other group of Christian believers, can individuals make fresh starts and feel safe enough to abandon old patterns of behaviour? With sufficient trust, we may allow others to unwrap aspects of ourselves we would rather keep hidden, and dare remove whatever covering may obscure our true identity. The group has a role in calling forth individual members like Lazarus from his tomb. Where the group is the tomb, however, we must believe that God grieves for us, that he is on our side, wanting as much as we do that our experience of being together should be one that is life-giving.

You may, of course, be tempted to say of the group, 'Let it rot!' Then the image of the untying of Lazarus stands as a challenge. As individuals we need, perhaps, to ask ourselves whether our presence has a binding or loosening, a deadening or animating effect on other people. We may even need to ask the more fundamental question that Jesus asked of Martha, because to believe that Jesus is the resurrection and the life is to be a person of unquenchable hope; someone who overcomes revulsion and braves scathing comments through the power of love; someone who always tries again and occasionally achieves the impossible; someone who, above all, makes God's reputation a higher priority than their own. There may be a very heavy stone barring the way to such a new mode of being. It is likely to be the stone of our pride, but it need not stop us.

FOR PERSONAL REFLECTION

The Prayer at the Tomb

Jesus looked upwards and said, 'Father, I thank you for having heard me. I knew that you always hear me' (Jn 11:41-42)

⚜ *Think back to a time in your life when someone really did 'hear' you or take what you were saying seriously. What was that like for you? Relive the moment with gratitude. Thank God that he hears you always.*

⚜ *Now it is your turn to 'hear' ... In what ways might God have 'spoken' to you today?*

⚜ *We may feel our own faith is weak. Jesus did not give up on the people who were with him. He prayed for them that they might believe. In a time of silence, allow Jesus to pray for you.*

FOR A GROUP EXERCISE

⚜ *Having read the Gospel passage aloud, disperse for a time of individual reflection. Imagine what it would be like if your group were making a completely new beginning. Allow your imagination to wander freely ... you are 'unbound' from all that has gone before, from all expectations and from all hindrances. How does it feel? What is different?*

⚜ *Return to the circle and invite each member in turn to share from their time of reflection. You may decide to set a time limit. Honour each individual sharing with a moment of silence before continuing.*

⚜ *When each has had their turn, consider together:*
  - *What may be stirring?*
  - *Is there a sense of hope in any of this?*
  - *To what extent could the impossible become possible?*

⚜ *End this time together by reading the Gospel passage once more. Invite each member to say a word or phrase that has resonated with them in some way.*

NINE

Faithfulness is of God

So from that day on they planned to put him to death. Jesus therefore no longer walked about openly among the Jews, but went from there to a town called Ephraim in the region near the wilderness; and he remained there with the disciples.

Now the Passover of the Jews was near, and many went up from the country to Jerusalem before the Passover to purify themselves. They were looking for Jesus and were asking one another as they stood in the temple, 'What do you think? Surely he will not come to the festival, will he?' Now the chief priests and the Pharisees had given orders that anyone who knew where Jesus was should let them know, so that they might arrest him.

Six days before the Passover Jesus came to Bethany, the home of Lazarus, whom he had raised from the dead. There they gave a dinner for him. Martha served, and Lazarus was one of those at the table with him ... When the great crowd of the Jews learned that he was there, they came not only because of Jesus but also to see Lazarus, whom he had raised from the dead. So the chief priests planned to put Lazarus to death as well, since it was on account of him that many of the Jews were deserting and were believing in Jesus. (Jn 11:53-57; 12:1-2, 9-11)

The whole country seemed to be abuzz with excitement in the weeks leading up to Passover, as people started getting ready to journey to Jerusalem. Every year they flocked to the city from far and wide. The newly built Temple complex was a thirty-five acre site designed to accommodate festival visitors from all over the empire who swelled the city's population at this time of year. The main gathering area was the Court of Gentiles, that is, the furthest point into which non-Jews might venture. As they made their way into the vast concourse, newly arrived visitors looked to see if Jesus had dared show his face. 'Will he come?' seems to have been the main topic of conversation among the crowds. Passover was always a nervous time for the Roman authorities, who drafted in extra troops from Caesarea on the coast for crowd control. This year the situation was more volatile than ever.

As always, great numbers began to arrive well before the festival in order to prepare themselves. You did not need to have done anything morally wrong to be 'unclean'; it was just that most people had taken care of their dead during the past year and needed to go through a seven-day ritual of purification before entering the Temple or eating the Passover lamb. So it was that in the lead-up to any feast, and especially in the week before Passover, there was always an enormous throng of people arriving in the city day after day, camping out in tents on the hillside or finding lodgings in outlying villages.

Despite the inevitability of his arrest, Jesus was ready to keep that same 'appointment' in Jerusalem. Saint John tells us that Jesus arrived six days before Passover. According to St John's Gospel he had been lying low since the miraculous happenings in Bethany, not beyond the Jordan where he was before, but north of Jerusalem in the town of Ephraim. Ephraim is often identified with a Palestinian Christian hill town, now known as Taybeh, which looks down over the desert wilderness. Perhaps Jesus fled here as a fugitive with his disciples or simply slipped away for a time of retreat. Everyone seemed aware that his appointed 'hour' was approaching, though no one really knew what that climax might turn out to be.

At least some of the disciples were still hoping that Jesus would allow himself to be propelled to power by the multitudes, foremost amongst them the two men Jesus had nicknamed 'Sons of Thunder'. James and John came to Jesus privately whilst they were on the road and asked to be his co-commanders when he came to power. An earthly throne, however, was not Jesus' intention and he made this very clear:

> ... he took the twelve disciples aside by themselves, and said to them on the way, 'See, we are going up to Jerusalem, and the Son of Man will be handed over to the chief priests and scribes, and they will condemn him to death; then they will hand him over to the Gentiles to be mocked and flogged and crucified' ... (Mt 20:17-19)

This clear statement from Jesus did not make for a happy journey by all accounts. Consternation and fear took hold. Saint Mark suggests that the disciples parted company at this time, though perhaps only to be less conspicuous: 'They were on the road, going up to Jerusalem, and Jesus was walking ahead of them ... those who followed were afraid' (Mk 10:32). The Synoptic Gospels describe how Jesus passed through Jericho and had to jostle his way through crowded streets. How tempting it would have been to turn against the stream of traffic in the direction of Galilee! Jesus, however, had set his face for Jerusalem, and the disciples – all of them eventually – allowed themselves to be swept along in the tide of people.

Jericho, that wealthy oasis in the desert, was a gathering place for pilgrims from the north and east. Galilean Jews came on foot. Leaving the territory of Galilee, they would travel down the east side of the Jordan Valley before crossing the river to Jericho. It was not the most direct route but few chose to walk through

Samaritan territory. Once in Jericho they would be joined by other groups of Jews from Perea (now Jordan) before setting off westwards for the uphill climb to Jerusalem itself.

The sheer numbers of travellers passing through Jericho must have offered Jesus and the disciples who were with him a degree of cover. A blind beggar at the city gate, however, started shouting at the top of his voice, 'Son of David, have mercy on me!' (Mk 10:48). Some attempted to quieten the man, presumably because he was attracting unwelcome attention, but Jesus paused, called him over and healed him. Able to see again, 'Blind' Bartimaeus joyfully joined the throng of people who accompanied Jesus as they began the long ascent.

The road rose three and a half thousand feet from the searing heat of the valley floor up to Jerusalem in the mountains. As they laboured up the twisting road it was customary for the crowd of pilgrims to sing psalms. These were the 'Songs of Ascents' or 'Songs of Steps', which we know as Psalms 120 to 134. It is easy to imagine how the rhythms and word-images encouraged pilgrims onwards when stretches of their uphill march grew arduous.

> *I lift up my eyes to the hills –*
> *from where will my help come?*
> *My help comes from the LORD,*
> *who made heaven and earth.*
> *He will not let your foot be moved;*
> *he who keeps you will not slumber.*
> *He who keeps Israel*
> *will neither slumber nor sleep.*
> *The LORD is your keeper;*
> *the LORD is your shade at your right hand.*
> *The sun shall not strike you by day,*
> *nor the moon by night.*

The Lord will keep you from all evil;
he will keep your life.
The Lord will keep
your going out and your coming in
from this time on and for evermore. (Ps 121)

For Jesus and the disciples on this particular Passover pilgrimage, the singing of these words must have seemed more poignant than ever.

By the time they approached Bethany, the pilgrims knew that their journey was nearing its end. Bethany was an insignificant place, but it was familiar to Galilean Jews, situated as it was close to the well-worn pilgrim path. There may have been a settlement of Galileans there and it is possible that Martha's family home regularly offered hospitality to pilgrims from the north. Many would continue on to Bethphage, then over the brow of the hill to camp out on the Mount of Olives or find accommodation in Jerusalem. Saint John's Gospel has it that Jesus chose to stay in Bethany and it was not long before 'the great crowd of the Jews learned that he was there'. (Jn 12:9)

Martha, Mary and Lazarus may have sensed that this would be their last time together. And so, 'There they gave a dinner for him. Martha served, and Lazarus was one of those at the table with him' (Jn 12:2). Two of the Gospels place the occasion at the house of Simon the Leper. To touch a diseased person was to render oneself 'unclean' and Jesus was a devout Jew. In view of the purification ritual that Jews were expected to perform in readiness for Passover, it therefore made this a controversial gathering. It sounds as though it might also have been a tense one. An argument ensued. It happened when Judas took exception to the expensive ointment that Mary 'wasted' in anointing Jesus. Not all the disciples may yet have arrived and there may have been some anxiety about whether or not those who followed behind were going to come at all.

There is something familiar about all this. Most groups have their late arrivals and those who do not turn up. Perhaps there is someone in your own group like Simon, whose presence attracts unwelcome publicity, or an angry figure like Judas who hides sadness under the guise of indignation. There may be someone startlingly unselfconscious like Mary, or loudly outspoken like Bartimaeus whom others would like to hush. There may be an 'otherworldly' person like Lazarus with one foot in heaven already, so to speak, and someone quite the opposite like the down-to-earth Martha, ever concerned about the practical details, working hard to get things right and making sure that everyone gets something to eat, even if she has to serve the food herself.

The important point is that Jesus felt entirely at home with them and, despite being at variance over a number of issues, these old friends still consented to come together. It would have been easier and safer for them to avoid one another's company, which is, sadly, what many groups do in times of crisis. Jesus offers us a model of faithfulness. With only days to live we find him fulfilling this most poignant of commitments: to keep Passover in Jerusalem as he must, in the full knowledge that, amongst the thousands of lambs they were bringing to the altar, that year he himself was going to be a sacrificial victim. As he made his way to Jerusalem, some Pharisees warned him that Herod meant to kill him. Jesus, however, was resolute: 'For today, tomorrow, and the next day I must be on my way, because it is impossible for a prophet to be killed away from Jerusalem' (Lk 13:33). Jerusalem was where the prophets had always come to die.

Keeping commitments is not something that is always treated with due seriousness, especially when it carries a personal cost.

Most people are well intentioned and make earnest promises, but the person who unfailingly does what he says he is going to do is a rarity. More interesting offers lure us away; lethargy disinclines us to stir ourselves; challenges that threaten our fragile ego may seem better avoided. The creeping malady of unreliability can be fatal for a group. Even in the good times a team needs to pull together; in times of crisis, depending upon one another assumes greater importance still. Bonds must first be forged, and in order to foster a spirit of unity it is vital to gather regularly, whether or not the experience proves pleasurable.

The Bethany gathering took the form of a meal, and the concept of a meal is central to Christian worship-life. It runs counter-culturally to the growing trend of family members eating meals in separate rooms while watching the television or going online. At least once in a while we must lay aside our personal preferences in the spirit of community. It is good to share, to be together, to dialogue with one another, to meet face to face.

The meal in Bethany was something of a farewell. The more famous 'Last Supper' for Jesus and his disciples was held some days later in a secret location in Jerusalem, the so-called 'Upper Room'. That too was a painful and poignant time. Judas could not sustain the level of commitment required to follow his master to the end and he slipped out to betray him as Jesus knew he would, yet it proved to be a meal so pivotal to their faith that Christians continue to celebrate it daily throughout the world in obedience to Jesus' command, 'Do this in remembrance of me' (Lk 22:19). It is a thanksgiving to God, a self-giving as well as a mutual sharing, a remembering and a looking forward, a time of the profoundest prayer and an act of the most loving service. Above all, it is an intimate encounter with Jesus present in the bread and wine, the one who feeds us with himself.

Meeting with Jesus around the table provides the model and inspiration for all other human encounters. We know that reverence is due to God, but Jesus reminds us how respectfully we should approach one another as well. He humbly drew lessons from what he had observed in the houses of the rich, advising us not to grab the best place at table and, on the occasion of the Last Supper, tying a towel around his own waist in order to wash guests' feet as he had seen servants do. These table gatherings were anything but introspective; responsive to the needs of the world around them, Judas' disappearance at the Last Supper attracted little attention because it was assumed that he would be going out as usual to share some of the food with others less fortunate.

Communal meals were occasions Jesus loved: 'I have eagerly desired to eat this Passover with you before I suffer' (Lk 22:15), he said to his friends. It was a time for honest exchange, a safe setting in which the deepest of personal concerns could be given voice: 'Jesus was troubled in spirit, and declared, "Very truly, I tell you, one of you will betray me"' (Jn 13:21). It was also a time of reassurance and mutual comforting: 'Do not let your hearts be troubled. Believe in God, believe also in me' (Jn 14:1). Ultimately it was an experience of oneness that could only be fully experienced in company with Christ. Jesus prayed: 'Holy Father, protect them in your name that you have given me, so that they may be one, as we are one' (Jn 17:11). Jesus is still praying that same prayer. Let us allow it to be fulfilled amongst us here.

FOR PERSONAL REFLECTION

A Song of Steps

I was glad when they said to me,
'Let us go to the house of the Lord!' (Ps 122:1)

- ⚜ *Take the opportunity to walk to your place of worship (if you are physically able) for at least part of the way. Make it a reflective experience. Feel the hardship if there is any and offer it to God.*
- ⚜ *Rekindle your desire simply to worship.*

FOR A GROUP EXERCISE

'There they gave a dinner for him' (Jn 12:2)

- ⚜ *Decide to have a meal together. Choose the place carefully, as it needs to be somewhere quiet enough to allow for a conversation that everyone can join in. As in Bethany, it might be an idea to meet somewhere different, somewhere that is 'neutral ground'.*
- ⚜ *Learn from the particulars of the Gospel passage. For example, plan the occasion together so that the responsibility does not fall to one person. Let everyone follow Martha's example in helping or serving.*
- ⚜ *Acknowledge the place of Christ among you by saying Grace before Meals.*

TEN

The Qualities of Leadership

When they were approaching Jerusalem, at Bethphage and Bethany, near the Mount of Olives, he sent two of his disciples and said to them, 'Go into the village ahead of you, and immediately as you enter it, you will find tied there a colt that has never been ridden; untie it and bring it. If anyone says to you, "Why are you doing this?" just say this, "The Lord needs it and will send it back here immediately."' They went away and found a colt tied near a door, outside in the street. As they were untying it, some of the bystanders said to them, 'What are you doing, untying the colt?' They told them what Jesus had said; and they allowed them to take it. Then they brought the colt to Jesus and threw their cloaks on it; and he sat on it. Many people spread their cloaks on the road, and others spread leafy branches that they had cut in the fields. Then those who went ahead and those who followed were shouting,

'Hosanna!
Blessed is the one who comes in the name of the Lord!
Blessed is the coming kingdom of our ancestor David!
Hosanna in the highest heaven!'

Then he entered Jerusalem and went into the temple; and when he had looked around at everything, as it was already late, he went out to Bethany with the twelve. (Mk 11:1-11)

There was nothing particularly humble about riding on a donkey. Jesus normally walked everywhere, and the horse was a military beast. Jesus was humble because riding a donkey conveyed a clear message that he came in peace. The image of a great white horse, its rider wearing crowns and leading the armies of heaven to battle, is a vision for the end of time. Jesus entered Jerusalem on a young ass that had not even been broken in.

This particular 'triumphal entry' of Jesus must therefore have seemed rather less than triumphal to those who accompanied him. Jesus reached Jerusalem late in the day, looked around, then simply went back to Bethany. Those who hoped he might take arms against the Roman occupying forces – and armed soldiers were everywhere to be seen in the city at Passover time – were to be disappointed. The campaign he was waging was a spiritual battle with humankind's archenemy, Satan, where victory was to be found in the heart's surrender.

Jesus was no warrior, but it did not make him any less a king. The royal entry into Jerusalem had begun even before he borrowed a donkey in Bethany. Back in Jericho, where crowds of festival pilgrims were gathering for the ascent, a blind beggar had loudly hailed him above the babble. He did not call out, 'Teacher!' or 'Master!' but 'Son of David!' It may have been a wheedling kind of flattery … or was he sensing similar qualities of leadership in Jesus, as in the legendary shepherd king and his wise son Solomon? Suddenly the Passover pilgrimage had become something of a royal progress.

His disciples had hoped that Jesus' 'final hour' might offer the prospect of a showdown with their enemies, but when Jesus spoke of the great glory ahead of him, he did not have political triumph in mind. His was the glory of completing all that God had asked of him, the trusting obedience of a Son who sought to please his Father above all else, the suffering that would reveal the limitless compassion of the Father-God for his world. Jesus was aware that he was walking to his death. What more kingly qualities could there be than to lay down his life for the cause of God's truth and to die for love of his people?

The idea of a servant king who washed his disciples' feet and surrendered to his enemies without a fight was not one the disciples found easy to accept. Their qualms echo our own inner struggle to conceive of Christ's kingship as something other than power. Beneath our readiness to fawn at celebrity lies an all-too-human need for reward and reflected glory. Study our prayer-life and we may discover how much the Christian still hankers after a God who fights our battles, the 'all mighty' whose will we seek to bend to our own.

No wonder Jesus resisted all attempts to make him king. He contested every attribution of earthly authority, even the courteous address of 'Good Master'. Because of its connotations, the title of Messiah was one with which he took particular care to disassociate himself: 'He said to them, "But who do you say that I am?" Peter answered, "The Messiah of God". He sternly ordered and commanded them not to tell anyone …' (Lk 9:20-21). It made Jesus a fugitive from his own more enthusiastic followers: 'When Jesus realised that they were about to come and take him by force to make him king, he withdrew again to the mountain by himself' (Jn 6:15). Glory, as far as Jesus was concerned, had nothing to do with the glint of weapons or the thrill of popularity.

It is ironic that, after his arrest, the Roman soldiers' parody of kingship unwittingly accorded with Jesus' own views about the vanity of power. They twisted thorns into a crown, placed a stick in his right hand and bowed in mockery. By his appearance and unwillingness to defend his cause, Pilate doubted whether Jesus posed any threat though he still asked nervously: 'Are you the King of the Jews? … So you are a king?' (Jn 18:33-37). What strength Jesus possessed was at the service of those who had no strength of their own:

Here is my servant, whom I uphold,
my chosen, in whom my soul delights ...
He will not cry or lift up his voice,
or make it heard in the street;
a bruised reed he will not break,
and a dimly burning wick he will not quench;
he will faithfully bring forth justice. (Is 42:1-3)

The Son of David was the shepherd king with a care for the downtrodden of this world. There would be no ranting oratory. All that Jesus could say in answer to Pilate's interrogation was, 'My kingdom is not from this world ... my kingdom is not from here' (Jn 18:36). It was not Jesus' poor command of Latin that prevented him from saying more, it was just that he did not speak the language of power. He was humble, not grandiose; he did not surround himself with men of influence or the trappings of privilege. We see him hailed as David's heir by a blind beggar and anointed by a woman thought to be of ill repute. No armed escort accompanied him in procession: instead, 'many ... women who had come up with him to Jerusalem' (Mk 15:41). It was a gentile who presented Jesus to the Jewish nation in loud proclamation, 'Here is your King!' (Jn 19:14) and had the words 'The King of the Jews' hung over Jesus' dying head in three languages in case, like him, anyone should be left in an agony of doubt.

It raises the question of what kind of leadership is appropriate to Christian groups. If coercion, oppression, self-aggrandisement and display are 'from this world', then Christian leadership must be characterised by consent, collaboration, beneficence and modesty. The shepherd must be self-forgetting and, if necessary, self-sacrificing. That will require such love for God and obedience to his will as takes us beyond the bounds of our natural courage. Leadership must be of a transfigured kind: like the whiteness of light between Moses the law-giver and Elijah the prophet, true glory is inextricable from uprightness and integrity. Jesus' dialogue with Pilate places the prophetic voice at the heart of kingship: 'You say that I am a king. For this I was born, and for this I came into the world, to testify to the truth' (Jn 18:37).

Paradoxically, it was because Jesus allowed his Father sovereignty over his life that he assumed true dignity: we too will only become a true leader when we have learned to obey. It was often noted that Jesus' natural authority was different from that of the scribes. It does not seem to have been based on formal learning or on social status, instead it was a 'presence' that sprang from who he was. Jesus did not only have authority, he conferred it on others, both formally and informally. His leadership was of the transformative kind. The woman at the well is only one of many whose encounter with Jesus made other people start listening to what they had to say. No one need be afraid of diminishing their own authority by empowering others.

In every member of our group there will be glimpses of the kingly traits of Jesus, and we must not snuff out our own little light when we find someone with more obvious qualities of leadership. Participative leadership works whether or not a group has a designated leader. A group will only function if everyone contributes their gifts and claims their own personal authority, not in competition but in a spirit of mutual encouragement. True leadership creates an environment in which people grow in stature and maturity; it does not subdue or infantilise. Jesus knew better than anyone the weaknesses of his disciples, yet he trusted them to act in his name.

But we are rushing on ... Jesus is still making his way up from Jericho, sombrely aware that this was his final Passover.

The crowd were nevertheless in festive mood. Saint Mark tells us that there were 'those who went ahead and those who followed' (Mk 11:9). Jesus was not at the head of an army but right in the midst of a more eclectic mix of people. We can imagine them pausing on the road while two disciples diverted into the hilltop village to fetch a donkey for him so that he could be seen above the crowd. Hearing the sound of psalm singing from a distance, the villagers of Bethany probably came out to watch. Some no doubt joined the throng as it made its way downhill towards the city.

Did Jesus have some special foreknowledge of a donkey awaiting him in Bethany? The place the Gospels described was, in reality, a small village by modern standards and he must have encountered every man, woman, child, dog and donkey on previous visits. Jesus was said to have been there only a few weeks before when Lazarus' sisters sent their urgent message. He may have seen the young ass tied to the door of the house at the end of the village street. His words, '... just say this, "The Lord needs it ..."' (Mk 11:3) sound like a message to someone Jesus already knew. If his friends in Bethany were Essenes, the donkey may have been communally owned and available for use whenever required. This donkey, however, was unbroken. He was not likely to offer anyone an easy ride.

The animal Jesus chose to bear him is a powerful image of Christian calling. It is true that donkeys will stubbornly refuse to be prodded or cajoled against their will; when they trust their owner, however, they are gentle, strong and hardworking. The donkey offers a metaphor for consecration to God's service. This particular one was a colt, that is, a male. We are not told whether it had been gelded. The uncastrated 'jack' ass is a notoriously unpredictable creature and frighteningly ferocious if he starts bucking, kicking and biting. Some say that for Jesus to ride safely into Jerusalem on an unbroken, ungelded donkey colt amidst noisy crowds waving branches was as much a miracle as walking on water.

We will never know whether Jesus' mount behaved himself. It is possible that the journey into Jerusalem was not the sedate plod we imagine ... or did the mere presence of Jesus have the same effect as his calming of the storm? Whenever the traits of a jackass are seen in us, and the gentlest disposition suddenly rears up in temper, Jesus whispers donkey language into our long ears. The Kingdom of God is a place of redemption and transformation for even the most 'difficult'. We are the very ones Jesus chooses to bear him in triumph.

Saint Luke tells us that as they left Bethany, Jerusalem suddenly came into view and the mood of the psalm-singing pilgrims soared at the spectacular sight laid out below them: 'As he was now approaching the path down from the Mount of Olives, the whole multitude of the disciples began to praise God joyfully with a loud voice for all the deeds of power that they had seen, saying, "Blessed is the king who comes in the name of the Lord! Peace in heaven, and glory in the highest heaven!"' (Lk 19:37-38). 'Hosanna!' the companions of Jesus cried out, as people traditionally did to greet festival pilgrims arriving into the city. It was a plea for salvation taken from Psalm 118:25 and meant 'Save us!' Never before had the cry conveyed such immediacy, such hope and expectancy. Some Pharisees amongst the pilgrims said nervously, 'Teacher, order your disciples to stop.' He answered, 'I tell you, if these were silent, the stones would shout out' (Lk 19:39-40).

There must come a time for us all when we can no longer conceal, either from ourselves or from others, whom we are or whom we are capable of becoming. The revelation of leadership qualities will always cause consternation in certain quarters. As

Jesus rode through the gate, 'the whole city was in turmoil', though not everyone knew who he was because Jerusalem was full of foreign visitors. 'Who is this?' (Mt 21:10) they all asked. That is a question we may need to ask of ourselves and of those others with whom we live or work.

FOR PERSONAL REFLECTION

The 'Hosanna' Meditation

⚜ *Imagine yourself in the village street in Bethany. Distant psalm singing announces that Jesus is coming. How does it feel as you wait in anticipation? Everyone begins to shout, 'Hosanna! Blessed is the one who comes in the name of the Lord!' (Mk 11:9-10). What greeting of your own do you want to cry out to him?*

⚜ *You notice the many visitors to Jerusalem who are camping out on the Mount of Olives during the Passover festival. They are running to meet the procession as it makes its way from Bethany. They begin placing their cloaks on the road to make a royal carpet as Jesus takes the downhill path towards the city.*

⚜ *Join them in your imagination. Lay before him whatever you wish to offer or need to relinquish ... some regret or shameful memory, a nagging pain, something that worries you, a dream or a longing ... How does it feel to lay this down in his path? Will it be trampled by hooves or will the shadow of Jesus transform it in some way?*

⚜ *What blessing do you ask of Jesus as he passes on his way?*

FOR A GROUP EXERCISE

᚛ *Gather as a group in a semi-circle around a flip chart. Begin by inviting someone to read the Gospel passage at the beginning of the chapter. Take a few moments of silence to reflect. From this and other Gospel passages:*

- *What kingly qualities did people see in Jesus?*
- *'Brainstorm' words and phrases and put them up on the flip chart. Write them randomly over the page.*
- *Take a few minutes of individual reflection to look at the completed page of kingly qualities:*
  - *Which qualities do we recognise in members of this group?*
  - *Are there any qualities that are lacking among the membership?*
  - *When everyone is ready, share your thoughts with the others.*
  - *What seems to be emerging here?*

᚛ *Conclude the gathering with a time of prayer. You may wish to use the following verses from Psalm 118:22-29. This was a psalm that looked forward to the coming of the Messiah. It would be recited at festival time and may have been the very hymn sung in the Upper Room by Jesus and his disciples after the Last Supper:*

*The stone that the builders rejected
has become the chief cornerstone.
This is the Lord's doing;
it is marvellous in our eyes.
This is the day that the Lord has made;
let us rejoice and be glad in it.
Save us, we beseech you, O Lord!
O Lord, we beseech you, give us success!
Blessed is the one who comes in the name of the Lord.
We bless you from the house of the Lord.*

The Lord is God,
and he has given us light.
Bind the festal procession with branches,
up to the horns of the altar.
You are my God, and I will give thanks to you;
you are my God, I will extol you.
O give thanks to the Lord, for he is good,
for his steadfast love endures forever.
Glory be ...

ELEVEN
Empathy Heals

*A leper came to him begging him, and kneeling he said to him,
'If you choose, you can make me clean.' Moved with pity, Jesus
stretched out his hand and touched him, and said to him, 'I do
choose. Be made clean!' Immediately the leprosy left him, and
he was made clean. After sternly warning him he sent him away
at once, saying to him, 'See that you say nothing to anyone;
but go, show yourself to the priest, and offer for your cleansing
what Moses commanded, as a testimony to them.' But he went
out and began to proclaim it freely, and to spread the word, so
that Jesus could no longer go into a town openly, but stayed out
in the country; and people came to him from every quarter.*
(Mk 1:40-46)

It may be fanciful to suppose that the leper Jesus encountered in
Galilee was the same 'Simon the Leper' whose hospitality Jesus
had accepted in Bethany. However there was only one Temple
and it was in Jerusalem, so when Jesus instructed the cured leper
to make the burnt offering as Moses stipulated, he was expecting
him to make that arduous journey south. It is not impossible
that he made his way to Jerusalem and settled down with other
Galileans or lepers living close to the city in Bethany where
Jesus encountered him again. It was here that St Mark's Gospel
situates the anointing story at the end of Jesus' ministry, 'While
he was at Bethany in the house of Simon the leper, as he sat at
the table' (Mk 14:3).

A cured leper asking the Temple priests for the ceremony of
ritual cleansing would have caused a considerable stir. This is

because until recent times leprosy had no cure. The cleansing ritual applied to a range of other skin complaints too, some of which might clear up of their own accord, but the excitement aroused by the news of this particular healing story suggests that the man did indeed suffer from the incurable leprous condition we now prefer to call Hansen's disease.

Though it progressed slowly over a number of years, the symptoms of leprosy were impossible to hide once the face had begun to show the characteristic whitened, deeply furrowed thickening of the skin. In advanced cases nerve damage could paralyse the face; there might be blindness; the nose might be lost. The voices of the ten lepers calling out, 'Jesus, Master, have mercy on us!' (Lk 17:13) would have been hoarse and rasping. Modern horror films about the so-called undead had their ancient counterpart in reality, for a leper in the advanced stages of the disease had the appearance of a living corpse, his filthy rags a shroud, the body decomposing whilst he still stumbled about. 'Foot drop' made it difficult to pick the feet up when walking, and eventually numbness of the extremities would reduce hands and feet to claws before they were worn away altogether, leaving just swollen stumps. Infected wounds and ulcers meant that a leper could be detected downwind by their smell. They were figures of dread. Total social rejection was the worst suffering of all.

Jesus must have known what he was asking of the leper. Ritual purification for the cleansing of someone cured of a skin disease was an expensive and lengthy process as laid down in Leviticus. First the priest had to make a physical examination. Two doves were then taken, one killed over a clay bowl of fresh spring water and the leper sprinkled seven times with the bloody liquid, the other dipped in the bowl and allowed to fly away. For the next seven days the leper was required to sleep in the open air, wash himself and his clothes, and shave all his body hair including beard and eyebrows. Clean and smooth as a newborn baby, the leper began life again. On the eighth day, three lambs were offered together with some fine flour and oil – one lamb as a holy gift for the priest, the others sacrificed for sins. The priest would dab blood and then oil on the lobe of the person's right ear, on the thumb of the right hand and on the big toe of the right foot. With whatever oil was left, the leper was anointed on the head. This completed the ceremony.

The applying of blood to the earlobe, thumb and big toe, and the anointing with oil, were the same rituals used to consecrate a priest. Together with the bathing and shaving, and the symbolic flight of the dove, it constituted a powerfully moving drama of the liberation from sin to become a new person made holy and consecrated to God's service. It is reminiscent of the sacraments of Baptism and Confirmation in our own Christian faith journey. No wonder Jesus stressed its importance as a testimony to God's compassion. It spoke of forgiveness, hope, cleansing and release. The Law was given in order to restore people's relationship with God and their neighbours; it was never intended to debar the majority of God's people from the worship life of the nation.

The phrase 'he went out and began to proclaim it freely' (Mk 1:45) suggests that the leper Jesus cured was now healthy enough in appearance to enter towns and villages without causing consternation. Jesus nevertheless knew that until the priests pronounced him clean, the leper was still officially prohibited from places of human habitation. The man called Simon who lived in Bethany continued to be known as 'the Leper', which suggests that however impossible the cure for leprosy, social acceptance remained more elusive still. You might say that this was the greater 'sign and wonder' – not that the leper was cured but that Jesus had been so willing to touch him in the first place.

In the days of Jesus, there was a supposed link between suffering and sinfulness, not a psychological one where feeling bad about yourself can affect your health. It was a more direct connection – all sickness was regarded as a punishment for sin, your own or the guilt of previous generations of your family. According to the Law, skin diseases and conditions with abnormal discharges rendered the sufferer ritually unclean, though it did not mean that they had necessarily sinned. The very poor – who were more likely to succumb to disease and were also more likely to have ancestors of mixed race – had less understanding of Hebrew and therefore of the Law. The sick poor were therefore generally all assumed to be sinners. Amongst the poor of Jesus' time was a prevailing sense that God had withdrawn his blessing, leaving them vulnerable to the merciless forces of evil. Consequently, when people came to him for healing, he would say, 'your sins are forgiven you' (Lk 5:20). He pronounced them clean and restored their hope in a God of love. By doing so, of course, he was in danger of being seen to take authority away from the Temple priests. He was also challenging social attitudes towards poverty. In effect, he was saying that affliction was not necessarily deserved; to be a sick person or a poor person was not the same as being a bad person.

Due to its disfiguring effects, leprosy was regarded with especial revulsion. The worse the suffering, the more deserving a person must be of punishment, or so it was thought. A leper could therefore expect little pity. Banished from human society and beyond the mercy of God, it is difficult to grasp the totality of a leper's abandonment. No wonder lepers gathered in colonies for mutual support. It was ten lepers who approached Jesus at the edge of a village on the border between Samaria and Galilee. Again Jesus told them: '"Go and show yourselves to the priests." And as they went, they were made clean' (Lk 17:13-14).

Near Jerusalem, lepers might discover others of their kind. The Temple Scroll from Qumran refers to a place for lepers east of Jerusalem, just beyond the three-thousand-cubit exclusion zone that kept them at a distance. Bethany, out of sight of the Temple, seems a likely location for such a colony where lepers could receive care, and St Mark's mention of Simon the Leper's home in Bethany adds weight to this. Some people go so far as to suggest that Lazarus may have been a leper too.

In view of Martha's usual hospitality, Simon the Leper's house was an odd choice of venue for a farewell meal. Even so, it demonstrates Jesus' attitude towards suffering. The passage about the healing of the Galilean leper describes Jesus as 'moved with pity' (Mk 1:41), though a minority of texts have it as 'moved with anger'. It is easy to see why the translators would prefer a response of compassion to a reaction of anger. Anger is difficult to comprehend in the context of a healing miracle. It suggests, perhaps, that Jesus was indignant at the leper's plight, horrified by how remotely this man's life resembled what God desires for humankind. It was a kind of compassion that goes beyond sympathy to share in the experience of another, including a sense of injustice that they may not necessarily feel for themselves.

For the leper to contravene the Law by drawing close to Jesus suggests an instinctive trust in his approachability, a nascent faith that had already begun to override the sense of God's mercilessness. He knelt before Jesus in an attitude of worship. His boldness is an encouragement for any of us who instinctively shrink from what is holy in our moments of shame. I imagine Jesus became deeply moved as the leper dropped to his knees before him, that he looked into his eyes with intense concern to examine the cause of his greatest suffering. The leper did not ask to be cured; it was forgiveness for which he was begging. 'If you choose,' he pleaded, 'you can make me clean.' I like to think that it was with a fierce earnestness that Jesus replied, 'I do choose. Be made clean!' (Mk 1:40-41).

The 'touch' of Jesus sounds as though it was warmer than a fleeting brush of the sleeve. This was the source of healing power, the awakening in the sufferer himself of belief in a God who cares. For in Jesus we begin to understand that God's loving-kindness is more than condescension bestowed from a sterile distance. Jesus appeared to be profoundly affected by a person's suffering. He seemed to understand how self-rejecting, shaming and abhorrent it might feel to believe oneself beyond the reach of God's mercy.

True empathy is to show sufficient understanding of all that another person is going through, in order that they no longer feel alone. It has a powerful healing effect. It explains why Jesus said, 'your faith has made you well' (Lk 17:19) to the ten lepers. The experience of God's benignity, or even that of other human beings, seems to kindle a regenerative potential within us that is normally damped down or extinguished altogether by the fatalism of our outlook. Believing in our own unlovability or in the unmitigated hostility of destiny, we succumb to misfortune by giving up on ourselves. It only takes something as simple as the touch of a hand for a very different kind of faith to emerge. Jesus was demonstrating to the marginalised of his society that God loved them as a father loves his 'little ones'. In doing so he challenged the exclusivity of the circle of people some Pharisees and priests regarded as righteous in the eyes of God.

It is a construct of the human mind that our fallibility imposes distance between God and us. On the contrary, his nature is to reach out. Jesus showed that God feels the pain of the least in society, as well as the downtrodden, those falsely accused, persecuted, in constant danger, hungry, marginalised and stripped of a future. In fact, the compassion of Jesus consigned him to the same fate. The Gospel passage tells us that he had to avoid towns and stay out in lonely places like lepers did. Taking refuge in the home of a leper is a powerful image of the extent to which Jesus eventually became an outcast himself.

We are left wondering, though, about the nature of the leper's healing. Did he experience a physical recovery, or was it that, still leprous in body, he felt restored in mind and spirit by God's forgiveness? By sending a still leprous man into the Temple precincts to ask for the cleansing ritual would be a dramatic challenge to conventional ideas linking sin and illness, yet it seems unlikely that Jesus would expose a friendless man to the full force of official hostility in order to make a point. The leper must have been whole and healthy when he set off for Jerusalem. As for the priests, we can only guess whether or not they were willing to officially release the leper from his sins.

Ritual laxity and disrespect for the Law were accusations hurled at Jesus on various occasions, though he was only ever opposed to the way the Law had come to be interpreted. Jesus criticised the process of accretion, whereby human regulations had come to be taught as though they were God's laws. What make a person unclean, he said, are not minor lapses in observance: 'It is what comes out of a person that defiles. For it is from within, from the human heart, that evil intentions come: fornication, theft, murder, adultery, avarice, wickedness, deceit, licentiousness, envy, slander, pride, folly' (Mk 7:20-22). How sad it is that we ourselves may still, consciously or unconsciously, divide people into 'clean' and 'unclean', and justify our disdain of those deemed to be 'unclean' by convincing ourselves that they deserve it. How tragic that we should withhold forgiveness from others and, by doing so, perhaps deny them life and health as well.

So often those who suffer believe that they deserve it. The sick people who came to Jesus acknowledged a sense of 'uncleanness', and the forgiveness Jesus offered released them from shame and freed them to thrive. His attitude sets an ideal before us of how to be in relationship; forgiveness is not about being prepared to overlook particular trespasses from a position of moral superiority, but about loving people into wholeness with an empathetic and non-judgemental mindset. Most people can and will change if we allow them to. By setting someone free from the condemnation we feel towards them in our hearts, we in some way 'cleanse' them, and feeling accepted may well be a healing experience for them in any number of ways. Who knows what miracles are possible? The first thing to change must be the way that we perceive other people. Until we heal our own attitudes we will never be healers of anyone else.

Assuming that the meal at Simon's house in Bethany, as narrated by St Matthew and St Mark, was the same occasion that St John described, Martha might have been a little put out that Jesus chose to eat at the leper's house rather than at hers. She nevertheless joined them there and served the meal. Nothing much has changed in the intervening years: Jesus still keeps company with those whom others shun, and that is where we will find him if we wish to share his table.

FOR PERSONAL REFLECTION

The Leper's House Prayer

'… *he was at Bethany in the house of Simon the leper*' (Mk 14:3)

- *The 'house' is often used as a spiritual metaphor for our inner self. Invite Jesus in. Thank him for anything that has been a good experience for you today.*

- *The leper's house was a place that no one else wanted to approach or enter. Perhaps there are things about you that keep others away or make you feel disgusted with yourself. Tell Jesus about them. Ask him to have compassion. Explore with him what makes you feel as you do.*

  Do not doubt that Jesus desires to make you clean and whole. 'I choose to' (Mk 1:41) he is saying to you. Imagine him stretching out his hand and touching you. Stay with that image.

FOR A GROUP EXERCISE

Gather in a circle. Discuss together:

- *Who are the 'lepers' of our modern society?*
- *How closely do we, or should we, associate with people who are rejected or marginalised by the rest of society?*
- *Does the experience of being in this group ever leave any member(s) feeling left out or shunned?*
- *What, if anything, needs to change?*

Say together these verses from Psalm 103:

> *Bless the LORD, O my soul,*
> *and all that is within me,*
> *bless his holy name.*

Bless the LORD, O my soul,
and do not forget all his benefits –
who forgives all your iniquity,
who heals all your diseases,
who redeems your life from the Pit,
who crowns you with steadfast love and mercy,
who satisfies you with good as long as you live
so that your youth is renewed like the eagle's.

The LORD works vindication
and justice for all who are oppressed.
He made known his ways to Moses,
his acts to the people of Israel.
The LORD is merciful and gracious,
slow to anger and abounding in steadfast love.
He will not always accuse,
nor will he keep his anger forever.
He does not deal with us according to our sins,
nor repay us according to our iniquities.
For as the heavens are high above the earth,
so great is his steadfast love towards those who fear him;
For he knows how we were made;
he remembers that we are dust.
as far as the east is from the west,
so far he removes our transgressions from us.
As a father has compassion for his children,
so the LORD has compassion for those who fear him.
For he knows how we were made;
he remembers that we are dust.
The steadfast love of the LORD is from everlasting to
everlasting
on those who fear him,
and his righteousness to children's children,
to those who keep his covenant
and remember to do his commandments.

🌱 *The verses describe God's compassionate nature. Consider whether the same can be said of ourselves in this group or community. Reflect on how comfortable would you feel replacing 'He' with 'I' in some of those verses?*

I am merciful and gracious,
Slow to anger and abounding in love.
I will not always accuse,
Nor will I keep being angry forever.
I do not always deal with people as they deserve,
Nor pay them back for what they have done.
For I know how they are made;
I remember that they are very fragile.

🌱 *You may wish to conclude with a time of prayer for the life of the group or community, remembering also those in our world who suffer.*

TWELVE

Time is a Precious Ointment

While he was at Bethany in the house of Simon the leper, as he sat at the table, a woman came with an alabaster jar of very costly ointment of nard, and she broke open the jar and poured the ointment on his head. But some were there who said to one another in anger, 'Why was the ointment wasted in this way? For this ointment could have been sold for more than three hundred denarii, and the money given to the poor.' And they scolded her. But Jesus said, 'Let her alone; why do you trouble her? She has performed a good service for me. For you always have the poor with you, and you can show kindness to them whenever you wish; but you will not always have me. She has done what she could; she has anointed my body beforehand for its burial. Truly I tell you, wherever the good news is proclaimed in the whole world, what she has done will be told in remembrance of her. (Mk 14:3-9)

Saint John's account of the story adds that the woman's name was Mary, the same Mary of Bethany who had sat at the feet of Jesus. On that occasion she had upset Martha; now she was upsetting other people. Mary seemed to have a knack for making people angry. She may anger us. We may feel a rising indignation whenever other people leave us to do all the work or waste money; we may feel embarrassed or even excluded when a couple in a public place seem absorbed in one another. We may therefore have already joined the chorus of people who 'scolded her' (Mk 14:5).

The disciples must have found it all the more irritating when Jesus once again rushed to her defence. More than that, he seemed to regard her wantonness as somehow encapsulating the Gospel. That message of good news had not always been understood or accepted. There could scarcely have been a single person of their nation who had failed to hear of Jesus, yet not all Jews believed that it was God who sent him. Some of his own disciples struggled with Jesus' image of a God who loves sinners and who favours the poor; many expected a Messiah, not a man of peace who was willing to surrender himself into the hands of his enemies. Mary of Bethany, on the other hand, did seem to understand the gospel of love. Wordlessly, she broke the jar and poured out its precious contents. It must have seemed to Jesus that he was watching the story of his whole life played out in a single symbolic gesture.

Mary's action clearly carried greater significance than a show of hospitality to an honoured guest. In her eyes, Jesus was the long-awaited 'Christ'. It was not for a warrior's strength or regal bearing that he was the Chosen One: 'the LORD does not see as mortals see,' God had said to Samuel, 'they look on the outward appearance, but the LORD looks on the heart' (1 Sm 16:7). Mary also looked on the heart, and recognised in Jesus' heart the limitless compassion of God. His disciples seemed more concerned with expense and protocol; they were aghast when Mary interrupted the men's conversation to imitate a priestly ritual:

> *I have found my servant David;*
> *with my holy oil I have anointed him;*
> *I will establish his line for ever,*
> *and his throne as long as the heavens endure.* (Ps 89:20, 29)

They would have been familiar with the story of King David, when God had instructed Samuel, 'Rise and anoint him; for this is the one.' At this, 'Samuel took the horn of oil, and anointed him in the presence of his brothers' (1 Sm 16:12-13). Mary was evidently saying of Jesus, 'This is the one!' to any of the disciples still in doubt.

Consciously or unconsciously, Mary was also preparing Jesus' body for burial. She must have realised that his death was fast approaching, though she could not have known that on that day there would be no one to perform this last act of love. We will never know whether her action was planned or spontaneous. What matters is that, at that moment, she was offering a most precious gift as an expression of devotion. Our self-surrender is the only appropriate human response to the incomprehensibly generous love of God. Jesus' statement 'you will not always have me' (Mk 14:7) reminds the task-driven amongst us that at the heart of our faith is a person.

This extraordinary scene in Bethany at the end of Jesus' life, set in the dinginess of a leper's hovel, has echoes of the poor stable at his birth. It was there that those other mystical figures, magi from the east, were said to have knelt in the straw to offer the Christ-child their precious gifts: gold in homage to a king; frankincense in adoration of a deity; myrrh for the burial of one who came to die. In Bethany, a group of beggars and fishermen, no more distinguished than the carpenter of Nazareth, watched wonderingly as Mary anointed her King, and faithfully prepared the Son of God for his death on a Cross.

Who was she, this prophetic figure? Mary and her Bethany family are a puzzling contradiction. The Gospels situate them in a leper village, yet pure spikenard from India is suggestive of fabulous wealth. The Gospel writers put the value of its contents at three hundred silver coins, nearly a whole year's wages. Mary's sister Martha was sufficiently socially assured to reprimand the Master on more than one occasion, and to discourse with him on resurrection. In a culture where it was unusual to remain unmarried, there is no mention of spouses. One explanation is that Lazarus may have suffered from a condition that required his two sisters to dedicate their lives to his care. Jesus told a parable about a leper called Lazarus who used to beg at a rich man's gate, his sores licked by dogs, but this profile scarcely fits Lazarus of Bethany who was universally mourned and whose family could afford to live lavishly.

If the family was rich, then Mary may have been relinquishing all that remained of some private inheritance. Yet the reaction of the people in the room suggests that the value of the ointment was common knowledge. Mary's emptying of the jar was unlikely to have aroused such outrage had it been hers to give away. One inescapable conclusion is that the precious ointment may not have been hers at all.

We are beginning to come closer, perhaps, to the truth about this mysteriously disparate collection of people in Bethany whose lives touched one another's so closely. There was within Judaism an ascetic movement of pious Jews who lived together in communities to pursue a life of prayer and meditation. Essenes, as they are known, were to be found in a number of locations, most famously in Qumran by the Dead Sea. It is believed that there may have been such a community in Bethany.

Essenes withdrew from Temple worship to seek what they saw as a purer way of life. They mostly avoided the bustle of cities for a life of seclusion while they awaited the coming of the Messiah. These 'brothers and sisters' – for they might include women – lived celibate lives for the most part. Each member devoted him or herself to some particular work. They renounced the use of money and held property in common. Meals were communal occasions, allowing for meaningful discourse on spiritual matters. It was their custom to reflect deeply on the scriptures. Essenes were known to be peace-loving, trustworthy, and affectionate to one another. Their focus was on charitable works for which each might draw from the common purse at their own discretion. The Essenes set up houses for the destitute, and it is possible that their colony in Bethany took in lepers.

It may be that Jesus was influenced by Essene ideas or that he rejoiced to find communities who shared his. Embroiled in public debates, gathering crowds about him and being described more as a winebibber than an ascetic, not everything about the Essene way of life resonates with Jesus' own, but we see the same compassion for the lost, the same renunciation of riches, the same brotherly love, and the same ideal of a simple life lived in common.

While uncomprehending outsiders were affronted by her action, it was natural that Jesus should have championed Mary, knowing that perfume in such quantity was likely to have been donated by some distinguished benefactor for the burial of the poor, and that this was her particular area of ministry. Jesus said, 'She has performed a good service for me' (Mk 14:6) meaning, perhaps, 'This is her work of charity'. She was preparing him for burial just as she may have buried many a poor man with no one else to mourn him.

Mary of Bethany expands our concept of what charity may be. The emotional toll of Jesus' last days cannot be underestimated. We who habitually petition him for help may struggle to conceive of Jesus as the needy one. There are various women mentioned in the Gospels who did understand the needs of Jesus and his companions: Mary of Magdala, Susanna, Joanna and many others, 'provided for them out of their resources' (Lk 8:3). Jesus' humanity is portrayed honestly in the Gospels. We see him not just hungry, thirsty and weary, but variously tearful, ecstatic, serene, angry, frustrated, moved and, on the night of his arrest, in a paralysing state of dread. We may be no more comfortable with the vulnerability of those with whom we live and work than we are with the humanity of Jesus. Attuned to the needy 'out there', we may sometimes be in danger of forgetting that our own close associates may also be suffering from self-doubt, loneliness and any number of anxieties, shames or sorrows.

Mary of Bethany's admiration for Jesus did not blind her to the emotional fragility of a man about to die. Aware of the unconditional self-sacrifice he was prepared to make, she cherished him and dared expose her own feelings in front of those she might expect to belittle her actions. Unlike those who judge by what they observe, Mary looked more deeply. She demonstrated that she valued Jesus, appreciated the significance of what he was doing and showed an understanding of what it was costing him. The gift of our time, presence and engagement with people is as great as any work of charity. For Mary, as for Jesus, self-gift was without reserve.

We are no doubt used to working hard and giving generously to good causes. What a pity if being truly present to other members of our own group, family or community was seen as 'wasting precious time that could have been given to the poor'. Time is the precious ointment we sometimes need to lavish upon one another. We do not have to wait until someone dies before we give their eulogy. We need to let them know how much they mean to us in advance of burial, as Mary did for Jesus. We might, for example, consider committing ourselves to a regular amount of time together as a group, not for business but purely out of friendship. No lavish displays of affection are required, just the communication of a little warmth, a mutual valuing of who we are and, as Mary did for Jesus, an acknowledgement of what each may be suffering or having to face.

This story of Mary and Jesus challenges us to recognise the personal struggles of those with whom we share our lives. Jesus' statement, 'you always have the poor with you, but you will not always have me' (Mt 26:11), could equally be said to us by any member of our community or family. It is not to encourage looking inwards, merely to cultivate a quality of community that really can support, inspire, inform and regenerate outreach.

You may have noticed that the anointing story offers a sequel to that episode in St Luke's Gospel in which Martha complained to Jesus about her sister Mary. In this subsequent narrative St John adds that, as before, it was Martha serving at table. The difference is that this time there was no protest – not from Martha, at any rate – when her sister Mary made an open show of devotion to the Lord. Perhaps she had come to realise that Mary had indeed chosen 'the better part'.

FOR PERSONAL REFLECTION

Praying with an Elderly or Sick Person

'The house was filled with the fragrance of the perfume' (Jn 12:3)

- *Find some aromatherapy oil or hand cream and offer to massage their hands. Make yourself comfortable because you need to take time over this. Use slow, gentle movements.*

- *While you are massaging, pray for them in the silence of your heart. Do not be embarrassed by silence ... it is not necessary to use words. If they make conversation, avoid talking about yourself. Try instead to show some understanding of how it might be for them.*

FOR A GROUP EXERCISE

'... a woman came with an alabaster jar of very costly ointment of nard, and she broke open the jar and poured the ointment on his head ...' (Mk 14:3)

❧ Gather in a circle and settle yourselves to hear the Gospel passage from the beginning of this chapter. Then take some time for individual reflection. Before moving away from the circle, agree how long you need for quiet time alone. Consider:

- What is it that you most value in each of the other members of your group?

- How much of a struggle do you imagine it is for them at times?

- What might you say to them by way of encouragement?

Return to the circle. With one person at a time in the role of recipient, other members of the group may like to offer some brief comments of affirmation, understanding or encouragement. The recipient should have a chance to respond.

❧ Conclude by reading together Psalm 133:

How very good and pleasant it is
when kindred live together in unity!
It is like the precious oil on the head,
running down upon the beard,
on the beard of Aaron,
running down over the collar of his robes.
It is like the dew of Hermon,
which falls on the mountains of Zion.
For there the LORD ordained his blessing,
life for evermore.
Glory be ...

❧ To finish, the group may decide to offer some spontaneous gesture of affection for one another, such as a hug or blessing.

THIRTEEN
Kissing the Traitor

Six days before the Passover Jesus came to Bethany, the home of Lazarus, whom he had raised from the dead. There they gave a dinner for him. Martha served, and Lazarus was one of those at the table with him. Mary took a pound of costly perfume made of pure nard, anointed Jesus' feet, and wiped them with her hair. The house was filled with the fragrance of the perfume. But Judas Iscariot, one of his disciples (the one who was about to betray him), said, 'Why was this perfume not sold for three hundred denarii and the money given to the poor?' (He said this not because he cared about the poor, but because he was a thief; he kept the common purse and used to steal what was put into it.) Jesus said, 'Leave her alone. She bought it so that she might keep it for the day of my burial. You always have the poor with you, but you do not always have me. (Jn 12:1-8)

Bethany means 'House of the Poor' or 'House of Affliction' and it may be that Lazarus, Martha and Mary ran some kind of refuge there. It would be characteristic of Jesus to head for a colony of sick and destitute people; he seemed as drawn to the ragged and outcast as they were to him. It was while Jesus was there that the humble dwelling became 'filled with the fragrance of the perfume' (Jn 12:4). It must have seemed to those who felt marginalised from Temple worship that, with such heavenly odour wafting all about, God had come to them instead.

Perhaps Judas failed to see that by identifying with a sector of society without hope, Jesus was helping the poor in a way that handouts of food or money could never do. The presence in their midst of such a celebrated holy man gave them the assurance of God's favour and conferred a dignity they had never felt before. Experiencing his care and attention, sensing it to be genuine, the unloved and unlovely loved him in return. For some, like Mary, devotion to Jesus knew no bounds.

It was as Mary tenderly anointed her Lord with fragrant oil that Judas issued his famous challenge, one that brought everyone 'back to earth' with a jolt: 'Why was this perfume not sold for three hundred denarii and the money given to the poor?' They were probably sitting in a poorhouse when he said it, a place where material need was all too apparent. Open-handedness to the poor and needy was demanded by the Law of Moses, and as though to endorse what Judas was saying, Jesus began quoting from the Book of Deuteronomy: 'there will never cease to be some in need on the earth ...' (15:11). He broke off mid-sentence to add '... but you do not always have me' (Jn 12:8).

However much Judas may have been claiming the moral high ground, by contrast with Mary's limitless generosity he understood 'gift' in more measured terms. He may already have regarded the intended use of expensive ointment for the burial of the sick poor as wasteful – to use it all up on one person left him aghast. The perfume could have fetched three hundred silver coins, precisely ten times more than a slave was valued according to the Book of Exodus. It was for that very sum of thirty pieces of silver that Judas was reputed to have sold Jesus to the chief priests. His value had evidently plummeted in Judas' eyes.

It had not always been so. Judas seems to have been in one of the inner circles of disciples, and was known for his generosity. After all, the disciples at the Last Supper assumed that he had slipped away from the table to share some of their food with the poor. It is difficult to reconcile a reputation for open-handedness with the image of a thief. Somebody 'on the make' was unlikely to have been attracted to a penniless band of preachers in the first place. It was said that 'he kept the common purse and used to steal what was put into it' (Jn 12:6) though the disciples recognised that it was Judas' role to 'buy what we need' (Jn 13:29). Jesus was referring to Judas when he observed, 'One of you is a devil' (Jn 6:70), yet he said much the same to Peter: 'Get behind me, Satan!' (Mt 16:23). Given his outspokenness over the ointment, Judas sounds principled and anything but secretive. He did not accuse Mary, he merely asked a question that, in itself, was not unjustified. Jesus rebuffed it good-naturedly enough and it opened up a dialogue that enlightened everyone present about the nature of Jesus' mission. There is no growth without challenge.

Saint John nevertheless associated challenge with betrayal, as we all tend to do. Thus it was that when Judas accused Mary of misappropriating ointment that some wealthy donor had presumably given for the burial of the poor, the Gospel writer in turn accused Judas of misappropriating donations to the common purse. Behaving defensively creates a climate in which people are afraid to question anything in case their own shortcomings are exposed. There must be a space for challenge in every group or community without the challenger being cast in the role of traitor. Judas did not make challenges because he was a traitor, he turned into a traitor because he felt increasingly out of tune with the movement. We too will make traitors of our challengers unless there is a climate of openness in which people's concerns are given serious attention.

It was perhaps because he held the purse strings that Judas had become unpopular with other disciples. The one with the money bag holds the power in any group, however onerous it may actually feel to shoulder that responsibility. For adults to be reduced to financial dependency on another, it may be disempowering, even infantilising. It can breed resentment, especially where the purse-holder is not very good at consulting others or does not regard it as necessary. We need to be accountable to one another and transparent in our dealings if we expect others to trust us fully. Hiding from the left hand what the right hand is doing may apply to personal donations, but it should not extend to communal funds.

There may have been additional trust issues where Judas was concerned. The name Iscariot has given rise to the theory that Judas was one of the Sicarii, a band of blade-carrying assassins. It is more likely that the name simply meant 'a man of Kerioth'. Kerioth was a Judean village some distance south of Jerusalem. If so, Judas must have stood apart from the other disciples who were Galileans from the north. People different from us make easy scapegoats. Even a different accent is enough to foster suspicion.

Judas may have been disillusioned with Jesus' unwillingness to be a Messiah who would rid the land of its Roman occupiers. If so, he was by no means the only one. Indeed, he might have been expected to applaud Mary's anointing of Jesus if he were actively promoting him as a future king. On the contrary, her action seems to have been the final straw as far as Judas was concerned. In the sharpness of his tone we detect an anxiety about the woman's attitude of exaggerated devotion. Attracted to Jesus by the purity of his religious ideals, Judas may have felt increasingly uncomfortable with his apparently blasphemous claims to be one with the Father. To hear Jesus speak of the Temple's destruction may also have been deeply troubling. As a Judean he would have been more familiar with Temple worship than the Galilean disciples, who stared wonderingly as though seeing it for the first time.

It is difficult to understand why he did not simply return to Kerioth. To remain in the close circle of Jesus suggests that Judas still believed in him. The disillusion of Judas, if that is what it was, may have been a sense that Jesus was not following the will of God. He may yet have hoped to awaken him to his duty or even to accelerate events that Jesus himself was reluctant to set in motion. It is equally possible that Judas had come to share the views of the priestly authorities about the danger posed by Jesus' radical ideas, or that he was simply trying to rescue Jesus from self-destruction. Perhaps the chief priests convinced Judas to hand him over by persuading him that it was a safe custody until the Passover crowds dispersed. He may even have believed that Jesus understood and tacitly approved of the efforts he was making to save his life. After all, had Jesus not said: 'Do quickly what you are going to do' (Jn 13:27)?

It is difficult otherwise to see why Judas should step forward to greet Jesus in the Garden of Gethsemane with a kiss of friendship. Jesus' trial and execution were very likely the unintended consequences of a more honourable intention on Judas' part. After all, he did not appear as a witness and throwing the thirty pieces of silver at the feet of the priests certainly sounds like an expression of disgust. Judas may have felt doubly betrayed: Jesus had disappointed him; the chief priests had played false. We can imagine how utterly alone he felt in what seemed like a duplicitous world. It is tempting to see Judas' suicide as the despair of an idealist rather than the remorse of a traitor.

Placing blame for the betrayal squarely on Judas must have been comforting to other disciples who had also disputed Jesus' ideals at various times. Peter denied ever knowing Jesus and 'not even his brothers believed in him' (Jn 7:5). Every group needs its scapegoats; casting someone in the role of Satan's accomplice no doubt helped Jesus' followers to feel better about their own part in his downfall. It prompts the question about the extent to which we too project our own treachery onto others in our group, and intentionally marginalise someone who is not like us. All of us are capable of distorting the reputation of another in a way that we delight to believe. What we may actually be creating is a myth about ourselves: we are rejecting those aspects we cannot bear to acknowledge by attributing them to someone else.

Saint John believed that Judas had always been a thief, and it makes uncomfortable reading for any of us who 'keep the common purse' in our group or community. The word 'thief' is not one we are ever likely to apply to ourselves, but it is a salutary reminder that everything we spend of shared resources is 'ours' rather than 'mine'. It was the woman's unilateral decision to use the perfume, as much as her extravagance with it, that seems to have riled those who witnessed the anointing of Jesus. On this occasion Jesus defended her action and there will be times when we have no option but to act on our own discretion. We are nevertheless answerable to one another. Transparency over the disbursal of communal funds remains an important principle.

Saint John's version of the story reads differently to that of St Matthew and St Mark: it is Jesus' feet, rather than his head, that Mary anoints. It sounds as though the dinner party that took place in Bethany might have become confused with a completely separate occasion, which St Luke recounts (Lk 7:36-50) in the house of Simon the Pharisee in some other place. Thus the chaste Mary of Bethany who prepared Jesus for burial becomes a repentant woman of ill repute who prostrates herself before Jesus, pouring perfume over his feet and wiping them with her uncovered hair in an attitude of self-abandonment.

Perhaps it does not matter too much which woman it was, for there is within us all a Mary of Bethany, respected for her charitable good works, and equally there is a shadow self. Like Judas, we are capable of selling Jesus cheap or, like Peter, pretending that we are not associated with him at all. We may, like the prostitute at Jesus' feet, set our own worth lower still.

It was never a question of whether Judas was guilty; whatever his motives, he did betray Jesus. Nor is there any doubt about our own failings, however hard we may try to justify ourselves. It is more a question of how we acknowledge and deal with our flawed nature. Judas deeply regretted the way he had treated Jesus, and threw his tainted earnings away in disgust before destroying himself in self-abhorrence. His shame brought him to despair. It was otherwise with the woman of ill repute. Her shame brought her to Jesus. She poured out her tainted earnings over the feet of Jesus and trusted that he would love her enough to forgive.

FOR PERSONAL REFLECTION

'The Perfume Prayer'

Something as seductive as perfume seemed a strangely inappropriate gift to offer, but Jesus did not bristle or recoil at Mary's approach. Spend a few minutes alone with Jesus.

- *In your imagination pour out at his feet anything that has touched and delighted you today, giving thanks for every precious moment.*
- *Pour out at his feet the things that have caused you to feel shame, and ask forgiveness.*
- *Pour out at his feet the things that have wounded, frightened or made you anxious.*
- *Hear Jesus defend you from accusation: 'Leave her alone!' (Jn 12:7).*
- *Hear Jesus defend others from any accusations you might make about them: 'Leave him/her/them alone!'*
- *What gift or grace do you ask of Jesus to help you face tomorrow with peace of mind?*

FOR A GROUP EXERCISE

Pieces of Silver

✤ *In the anointing scene at Bethany we see different attitudes towards money. Mary seemed unconcerned about how much the perfume cost and used it generously, though she was accused of wastefulness. Judas, on the other hand, wanted to see a more responsible use of something that cost so much money, though he was accused of hypocrisy and greed.*

Put up a large piece of paper at one side of the room with SPENDING CAUTIOUSLY written on it, and, at the other side of the room, another piece of paper with SPENDING FREELY on it.

Invite the members of the group to reflect for a few moments about the way they approach their personal spending. There is no judgement involved; it is no less virtuous to be thrifty as it is to be open-handed. Invite everyone to place their chairs at the point they would locate themselves on the imaginary line between these two positions. Take a moment to observe the overall arrangement. Each person might like to say why they sat where they did or how easy or difficult it was to decide.

Now pull your chairs into a circle to discuss your shared resources:

- *Where on the line is it right for the group to be?*
- *How possible is that?*
- *What wisdom does Jesus offer?*
- *What prayer is beginning to emerge?*

You may find it helpful to read aloud Psalm 41 as part of a time of prayer together:

Happy are those who consider the poor;
the Lord delivers them in the day of trouble.
The Lord protects them and keeps them alive;
they are called happy in the land.

You do not give them up to the will of their enemies.
The LORD sustains them on their sickbed;
in their illness you heal all their infirmities.
As for me, I said, 'O LORD, be gracious to me;
heal me, for I have sinned against you.'
My enemies wonder in malice
when I will die, and my name perish.
And when they come to see me, they utter empty words,
while their hearts gather mischief;
when they go out, they tell it abroad.
All who hate me whisper together about me;
they imagine the worst for me.
They think that a deadly thing has fastened on me,
that I will not rise again from where I lie.
Even my bosom friend in whom I trusted,
who ate of my bread, has lifted the heel against me.
But you, O LORD, be gracious to me,
and raise me up, that I may repay them.
By this I know that you are pleased with me;
because my enemy has not triumphed over me.
But you have upheld me because of my integrity,
and set me in your presence for ever.
Blessed be the LORD, the God of Israel,
from everlasting to everlasting.
Amen and Amen.

FOURTEEN
From Where We Stand

When he had said this, as they were watching, he was lifted up,
and a cloud took him out of their sight. While he was going
and they were gazing up towards heaven, suddenly two men in
white robes stood by them. They said, 'Men of Galilee, why do
you stand looking up towards heaven? This Jesus, who has been
taken up from you into heaven, will come in the same way as
you saw him go into heaven.' (Acts 1:9-11)

King Herod the Great's construction projects were on a
breathtaking scale. In order to enlarge and embellish the Temple
in Jerusalem, for example, he remodelled an entire mountain.
So ambitious was the scheme that pious Jews worried he might
never accomplish it, leaving them without any Temple at all. They
need not have worried. The Temple itself was successfully rebuilt
without any disruption to daily worship, even if the rest of the
complex had still to be completed after King Herod's death.

The Temple area therefore remained something of a building
site throughout Jesus' lifetime, as it had been throughout the
lifetime of his parents. The colossal edifice dominated Jerusalem,
constructed on a vast platform atop Mount Moriah from stones of
astonishing size, with viaducts spanning the Tyropoeon Valley to
the city beyond. Those entering the Temple from the south climbed
stairways through candle-lit tunnels to emerge into the dazzling
sunlight of the plaza. The immense open space was enclosed by
marble colonnaded cloisters, with roof beams of carved cedar.
It was here in this outer court, where curious Gentiles rubbed
shoulders with observant Jews, that Jesus came each day to teach.

Only Jews might enter the inner courts. There, sacrificial offerings were burned on an outdoor altar before the imposing Temple building, which was mostly the preserve of priests. Within it was the Holy of Holies, where the unseen God had his earthly dwelling-place. Only the High Priest might cross its threshold and this occurred just once a year on the Day of Atonement. The Temple exterior was of shining white marble with a spiked golden roof to prevent birds from soiling it. With its tall bronze entrance doors, the Temple was a blinding spectacle in the brightness of the mountaintop sunshine. From the Mount of Olives across the valley you could see the glint of gold and catch whiffs of incense and burning fat as the smoke of burnt offerings rose high into the atmosphere.

The disciples were utterly taken in by the Temple's immensity and magnificence. Like us, perhaps, they judged by reputation and outward appearance. 'Look, Teacher!' they said, 'What large stones and what large buildings!' (Mk 13:1). Jesus seemed drawn to what remained of the original Temple, that is, Solomon's Porch, and it was here in the outer courts of the Temple complex that he chose to do his teaching. As for the grand new buildings, which drew the admiration of visitors from across the known world, he was heard to say that the whole structure was doomed: 'Do you see these great buildings? Not one stone will be left here upon another; all will be thrown down' (Mk 13:2).

Disturbed by his very different perspective, the leading disciples wanted to know what he meant by his remarks: 'When he was sitting on the Mount of Olives opposite the temple, Peter, James, John, and Andrew asked him privately' (Mk 13:3). It was too much to believe that King Herod's Temple could ever be destroyed, but destroyed it was, some forty years later, just as King Solomon's earlier Temple on the same site had also been destroyed.

The glory of that first Temple had consisted in something quite other than its scale or intricacy of design. Solomon had built a house in which God might dwell. It was not to immortalise his own name, as Herod seemed to be trying to do. The pillar of cloud that signified the presence of the Lord, which had guided the wandering Israelites through the wilderness, and which covered the Tent of Meeting where Moses talked with God, would now fill the house that Solomon built for him. No wonder the Jewish people felt utterly desolate when the Chaldeans destroyed that first Temple. Though the generation of returning exiles hurriedly rebuilt it, the second Temple did not look or feel the same, which was why Herod felt the need to embellish it. Architecturally it compared badly: the Ark of the Covenant containing the tablets of stone had gone; so, it was feared, had the bright cloud of God's glory. The prophet Ezekiel watched as God's presence departed: 'the glory of the LORD ascended from the middle of the city, and stopped on the mountain east of the city' (Ez 11:23).

Thus the Mount of Olives acquired its own sacred story as the place east of the city where the presence of God had been 'seen' to pause. It was not difficult to envision God resting amongst its olive groves in this evocative landscape, where a heavy cloud of mist rises up the sides of the mountainside by night and melts away with the morning sunshine. It was here on this same gentle green mount that Jesus used to retire for the night when he came to Jerusalem for the Jewish festivals. Saint Luke tells us that, 'Every day he was teaching in the temple, and at night he would go out and spend the night on the Mount of Olives, as it was called' (Lk 21:37). What people encountered on the slopes of Olivet in his company was something unaccountably holy and healing.

The Mount of Olives stands slightly higher than the city itself, separated from it by a rocky gorge but close enough for the massive walls and gateways of the newly embellished Herodian Temple to have dominated the view. The Mount of Olives offered a perspective that was more than visual. It was here that Jesus shared with the disciples his prophetic vision of times to come. During this 'Olivet Discourse', as it has come to be known, he described wars, earthquakes, famine, persecution, betrayal and false Messiahs. He also spoke of a glorious liberation in the fullness of time.

The exact place where Jesus shared these both harrowing and inspiring premonitions was, by tradition, a cave on the upper slopes of the Mount of Olives looking towards the city. A church has been built over the holy site, the Sanctuary of the Eleona. Here he prophesied the destruction of Jerusalem and tried to expand the disciples' understanding of God's Kingdom to conceive of a dimension beyond some earthly state with geographical boundaries. The Kingdom he proclaimed was within their reach. He imparted to them his own longing for God to reign over the hearts of men and women. It is said that when his disciples asked Jesus how to pray, it was here in this cave that they first heard the words of longing, 'Our Father in heaven, hallowed be your name. Your kingdom come. Your will be done, on earth as it is in heaven' (Mt 6:9-10). Bringing heaven to earth was what Jesus seemed to be doing by his very presence.

Descending the slopes of the Mount of Olives on a donkey as his followers spread palms before his passing feet, Jesus wept for the city, saying, 'If you, even you, had only recognised on this day the things that make for peace! But now they are hidden from your eyes ... they will not leave within you one stone upon another; because you did not recognise the time of your visitation from God' (Lk 19:41-44). Are we any better at recognising those moments when God comes to us? Jesus may or may not have known precisely what future historical events would lead to the destruction of Jerusalem, but he did understand the devastating consequences of resisting the movement of God in our lives. Whenever we do, it is a denial of reality, a refusal to see the danger we are in. More than that, it is a closing off to possibility.

Jesus identified truth as a way of being with life itself. 'I am the way, the truth and the life,' he said, as though these were somehow synonymous. He warned his followers against the 'blindness' to truth of the Pharisees. Jesus' way was to engage with reality, however painful it might feel. The events that took place at various locations on the Mount of Olives epitomise that unblinking candour and integrity of Jesus. Conflict, illness, disfigurement and death were all to be encountered there: it was in Bethany over the crest of the hill that he rolled away the stone from a stinking tomb in order to raise Lazarus to life; it was in the Garden of Gethsemane at the foot of the mount that he personally experienced all the anguish of a man about to be crucified. For Jesus, self-deception was not the way, nor any kind of life.

As for us, we prefer not to think about evil or death. Because we hesitate to believe that God's sovereignty extends over the very things of which we are most afraid, we develop a kind of myopia that distorts reality to fit into a fanciful world of our own construction. Who cannot sympathise with the two sets of brothers who took issue with Jesus over his prediction of the Temple's destruction? While its strength and splendour filled their gaze as they looked out from the Mount of Olives, they did not have to see what lay behind them over the crest of the hill: the wilderness of sun-scorched hills descending towards that blue strip on the horizon – earth's lowest place, the Dead Sea, devoid of plants or fish. The Mount of Olives stood symbolically between the earthly dwelling of the living God and the lifeless, watery realm of supposed evil. It offered a panorama of the whole of life, good and bad, inspiring and terrifying. Bethany was located here.

Most of us prefer not to linger in such a place. We avert our eyes from the shadier side of our own personalities and from the shortcomings of the institutions to which we belong, rather than welcome truth. Thus, we close the door on the God who comes to visit us with healing. Our relationships are hampered by the habit of revealing to others only part of the person we are, or by disguising our truest selves behind masks of piety, jollity or bravado. We shrink in shame from exposing our inadequacies. We hide them even from ourselves. By acting a part we are not truly 'present' to those with whom we share our life. God is a God of self-revelation whose name 'I AM who I AM' contrasts with our own lack of transparency. 'I am not who I say I am' is so often the way we present ourselves to others. The 'cloud' that signified the presence of God was an intense brightness, not an obscurity. To stand before God is to be rendered transparent before truth. It is not an exposure we need fear.

If our heavenly Father looks upon us with a loving gaze, it is all the more important that we should look with a loving gaze upon one another. In an environment of acceptance, where no one needs to put on a false persona in order to secure approval, we could all be naturally, unassumingly, authentically who we really are. We could let down our guardedness. We could inhabit the moment instead of hiding in the past or rushing towards the future. Our friends might find us humbler, less anxious, less peevish, less self-advertising. To be known and loved is the bedrock. Secure in ourselves, freed from self-absorption, we might listen with loving attention instead of with competitive intent. We would not only be more truly 'present', we might become more fully alive. To believe in the Resurrection of Jesus is to take hold of a quality of life that bursts through the constraints of what is usual or considered possible.

Bethany lay just over the crest of the Mount of Olives, where heaven had never seemed very remote from everyday experience. Their village close to Jerusalem may have been just out of sight of the Temple, which Jews had always associated with God's presence, yet Jesus had often passed that way. He had feasted there and rested there; he had freely availed of its figs and donkey knowing that what was 'theirs' was 'his'; he had accepted invitations to share a table with its lepers and allowed the marginalised – including women – to approach his person. He brought life and hope. God had come amongst his people. Earth was indeed 'as it is in heaven' in the company of Jesus. It therefore comes as no surprise that Bethany, the place where Jesus routinely blended into our human ordinariness, was where he eventually blurred from sight altogether. It all seemed to happen so simply and naturally:

... he led them out as far as Bethany, and, lifting up his hands, he blessed them. While he was blessing them, he withdrew from them and was carried up into heaven. And they worshipped him, and returned to Jerusalem with great joy; and they were continually in the temple blessing God. (Lk 24:50-53)

Recalling other agonising separations in our own experience, the reader may feel puzzled at the disciples' sense of joy, yet in this momentous overturning of expectations, absence had become the threshold of a more profound presence. The blessing of Jesus made 'being with' no longer dependent upon physical attendance. 'I am with you always' (Mt 28:20), he promised his disciples, and St Luke's description of the Ascension attests to a deep, abiding, intimate and energising experience of Jesus in which constant visibility is no longer necessary for any of us to feel contented and secure. 'Although you have not seen him, you love him; and even though you do not see him now, you believe in him and rejoice with an indescribable and glorious joy' (1 Pt 1:8).

Those who struggle with relationships will know that spending longer and longer hours in a person's company does not guarantee any greater sense of connectedness or security. Distrusting the faithfulness of the other, not daring to believe in our own lovability, we may test and pester our friends and partners for tokens of affection. Sometimes no amount of assurance suffices. It was otherwise with Jesus and his disciples. Their most fulfilling experience of him occurred at that moment when the distinction between physical presence and absence was lost. His body was no longer there yet his Spirit filled them. Together the disciples became – as we may – his Bethany, his home, the temple he so loved. It is the profoundest source of comfort to realise that closeness is not always a matter of distance and that the place we go to when we die is neither unfamiliar nor faraway.

Angels have long been trying to convey to humans how little distance there need be between earth and heaven, but our thinking is as structural as King Herod's viaducts – we can only think in terms of some deep gorge or limitless void to be spanned by heroic virtue. The written evidence of St Luke in the Acts of the Apostles suggests that the Ascension was more a kind of reduced visibility than any loss of presence. Jesus was no less there. Meanwhile, we strain our eyes to retain what is more reassuringly concrete. The angels chide us as they chided the disciples. Their 'seeing beyond' is not to see further, but more trustingly. Theirs is to feel earth suffused with heaven, to occupy a continuum where God's presence is not somewhere other than where you happen to be.

Meanwhile in Bethany, the disciples fell prostrate before their ascended Lord in adoration, thanksgiving and utter joy. Thanksgiving is perhaps the ultimate sense of perspective, one that rejoices in a more glorious reality than what may be immediately apparent. We are not asked to be mystics who see further than the limit of our eyesight, but to experience to the full what is 'here' and 'now' and to believe in the promise of a yet fuller life to come. It can only happen when we begin to entrust everything to God's love for safekeeping. Then we can cast our eyes towards a vision of 'beyond' that has, all this time, been directly in front of us, even in those aspects of our lives that we would rather not see at all. 'On earth as it is in heaven' has potential to be far more than just a muttered formula in our daily prayer.

FOR PERSONAL REFLECTION

The 'Mount of Olives' Prayer

'Then he led them out as far as Bethany, and, lifting up his hands, he blessed them.' (Lk 24:50)

- *Allow Jesus to lead you out to a place of quiet and safety. It may be in your imagination or you may wish to retreat to some peaceful place you know. 'View' the panorama of your life as it is at the moment. What do you 'see'? Point out the 'landmarks' to Jesus. Share with him the less pleasant views.*

- *Give him thanks for everything that makes you feel loved or gives you hope or that deepens your faith. Linger there. Allow joy to find a place in your heart.*

- *Pray for the grace you need. Ask him to raise his hands over you and to bless you.*

FOR A GROUP EXERCISE

❧ *Gather in a circle to commit this time to God. Agree how long you would like to spend on the following exercise. After reading the Gospel passage aloud, spend a few minutes in silence to reflect on your life together as a group or community.*

❧ *Below are some of the locations on the Mount of Olives that Jesus knew well. They symbolise our experience. Where do you think your group is at this time?*

- **Bethany**, *a place of ascension ... symbolises an ability to let go; the assurance of God's approachability and friendship; a wider perspective; openness to both reality and to potential; an ending that turns out to be a new beginning. It is characterised by loss, blurring, change, joy, hope, transformation, blessing and thanksgiving.*

- **The Cave**, *a place of shelter ... where Jesus taught his disciples the Lord's Prayer and where he shared with them the tribulations that were to come. The Cave symbolises a time of preparation; a regenerative experience; a maturing of ideas; the struggle to accept what must be; a desire to learn; a return to basics. It is characterised by darkness, questioning, confusion, challenge, indignation, honesty, prayerfulness, reflection and togetherness.*

- **The Garden**, *a place of agony ... where Jesus prayed and sweated blood as he awaited his arrest. The Garden symbolises the falseness of friends; pleading with God; dread of future change; doubts about one's personal capacity to cope. It is characterised by fear, loneliness, brokenness, recrimination, running away, drowsiness, violent reactions, painful surrender to the will of God, courage and sacrifice.*

- **The Necropolis**, *a place of deadness ... The sepulchres on the lower slopes of the Mount of Olives, whitewashed every year, occupied a prime position opposite the Temple. The*

Necropolis symbolises the keeping up of outward appearance, assumptions about God's favour, the importance of status and idealisation of the past. It is characterised by inertia, monotony, complacency, pride, uniformity, a strong sense of identity and peace.

✢ *As you come back together as a group, let each member in turn share their thoughts, uninterrupted, until everyone has had a chance to speak. Allow a broader discussion to develop so that the group can work towards a general consensus of where they might be at the moment. Then consider together:*

- *Where do you want to be?*
- *What needs to happen first?*
- *What prayer is emerging?*
- *You may like to finish with a time of prayer together, before closing with the Our Father.*

Conclusion

You may have heard the story about St John the Evangelist and how, in his final years, he had to be carried to church. The people of Ephesus were eager for some uplifting words from his venerable lips, but all he would say was: 'Little children, love one another!' Tiring of it, they asked why he kept repeating the same thing. 'Because,' he replied, 'the Lord commanded it … because this alone, if it is done, is sufficient, quite sufficient' (Jerome, *Commentary on Galatians*, III, 6).

Christians loving one another – is this what we have been encountering in these chapters? On the face of it, it seems not. According to Gospel accounts, Bethany was the scene of heated disagreements about money and propriety, of angry recriminations when people failed to do their share of the work or to turn up on time. It was in Bethany that Jesus, accused of letting his friend down, broke down in tears; it was from Bethany that he was sent out on an empty stomach. Everyday life in Bethany appears to have fallen remarkably short of the ideal set before us in the 'new commandment' of Jesus: 'Just as I have loved you, you also should love one another' (Jn 13:34).

The word 'love' is broad in meaning, and it is natural to assume that we have failed the Lord whenever we lack warmth towards another. Saint John the Evangelist knew very well that feelings are not made to order. What is conveyed by *agapate*, the Greek for 'be ye loving', is more a reframing of the way we think. Our outlook determines the way we behave towards people, and our deeds are what count.

Jesus' love was compassionate, though not necessarily fond. He simply related to people in a way that was uncompetitive and accepting. His was an active concern for all who came his way, a positive discrimination towards those whom the world rejected, the kind of beneficence that set no conditions and sought no reward. Though there might be little visible evidence of it, loving as he loved was based on a resolute belief in people's worth. He forgave and forgave again. It did not matter that people may not always deserve, appreciate or reciprocate his magnanimity. Out of love he was prepared even to die.

Neither should we make the showing of respect conditional. It is to do the right thing by other people, always. Loving as Jesus loved is to be consistently and universally fair, regardless of how we feel about them or whether it is in our interest or not. To love as Jesus loved was to feel the full wrath of Martha and reciprocate with tender solicitude; to come back for Lazarus rather than stay safe; to put his own good name at risk in defence of Mary. It was in Bethany as much as anywhere that we come to understand what it means 'to love as Jesus loved'. It was from here that he looked longingly upon Jerusalem, and wept for the very people he knew would nail him to a cross.

Are we ourselves capable of loving as non-defensively? We are. The real question is whether we are willing to try. On it depends our own inner peace, as well as the health of our relationships. More crucially, it is what marks us out as disciples of Jesus. Unity is at the heart of evangelisation.

Our oneness will remain a 'work in progress', and we must not despair at how slow that progress may seem. Relationships in Bethany were no easier than our own. At no point, however, did Jesus reject any of his disciples in favour of new ones, or find an alternative place to stay when he came up to Jerusalem. He simply continued to love those the Father had given him. 'They were yours, and you gave them to me' (Jn 17:6), he prayed.

The people with whom we live and work are God's gift to us. In ways we may find hard to comprehend, *all* those who share our lives are 'just what we need'. Learning to prize God's gifts will surely prove regenerative, and not just for ourselves. It was 'so that the world may believe' (Jn 17:21) that Jesus prayed his disciples might be one. It is still his prayer. Let it be ours.

That we may choose the one thing necessary,
Martha of Bethany, pray with us.

That our love for one another may fragrance our world,
Mary of Bethany, pray with us.

That we may be set free from all that binds us,
Lazarus of Bethany, pray with us.

That no one in our company may ever feel outcast again,
Simon, leper of Bethany, pray with us.